Reckoning X
Electronic Edition: January 2026

Reckoning *is a communal effort,*
and Reckoning X *was edited collectively.*
Editorial staff, in alphabetical order:

C.G. Aubrey
E.C. Barrett
Octavia Cade
Priya Chand
Offor Chidera
Michael J. DeLuca
Tim Fab-Eme
Joseph Hope
Kat Murray
Ruth Joffre
Aaron Kling
Andrew Kozma
Ellis Nye
Guillermo G. Mendoza
Jackie Roberti
Catherine Rockwood
Bernie Jean Schiebeling

Cover artwork "Circle of Life" and
text ornament by Mónica Robles Corzo
Endpaper artwork "Creation" by Daphne Fauber

Reckoning Press
206 East Flint Street
Lake Orion, MI 48362
www.reckoning.press
distributed by IngramSpark
Contents © 2026 by the authors and artists.
All rights reserved. ISSN 2474-7327
e-ISBN 978-1-955360-15-9
print ISBN 978-1-955360-14-2

Reckoning X

Contents

Cover: **Circle of Life**

Mónica Robles Corzo

Mónica Robles Corzo: creature designer, concept artist and illustrator. Onyx Equinox/Aztec Batman/En Casa Monstruos/Criterion Collection. Instagram: @monarobot

Endpaper: **Creation**

Daphne Fauber

Daphne Fauber (she/her) is a queer writer, Best of the Net nominated artist, and microbiologist transplanted from Indiana to Boston. When not reading books or agar plates, she can be found playing too many video games. Her work has been published in the *Brave New Girls* anthology, *Permafrost Magazine*, *Diet Milk Magazine*, and Pile Press, among others. She can be found on Instagram at @daphne.writes or at her website www.dank.pizza.

Editorial: **Circle of Life**

Michael J. DeLuca

"Everything's environmental justice" is something I used to say around the shop back during *Reckoning 2* or thereabouts, a way of indicating what kinds of environmental writing should go in the magazine: all kinds, from everywhere and everyone.

Ten years in, I stand by that statement, even as I acknowledge that "everywhere" for our purposes refers, with far too few exceptions, to the English-speaking world, and "everyone" means specifically those in earnest about enacting environmental justice, large-scale or small.

Let me put the lens of environmental justice over this book or device you're gazing into, *Reckoning X*, our collectively edited communication issue. This lens is many-leaved. Perhaps a very, very thin leaf is made from cobalt mined by children. Accessibility, access to information, access to services, education, cost, economic situation, race, nationality, sexuality, and ethnicity: these are all leaves of the environmental justice lens, as are the physical ones inside our heads made for us by some billions of years of evolution and, depending who you are and how you look, God.

Everything's communication, too. All behavior is communication. Mycelial networks, spores, the chemical interactions of root systems, birds dancing, orcas wearing salmon hats, cephalopod color displays, cat hackles, pheromones, ant chemical highways, ultraviolet floral pigmentation, and pretty much everything humans do, for better or worse. Communication is at the heart of environmental justice, and it's the heart of *Reckoning*. Who gets justice, who is even allowed to work for it, is a matter of who's allowed to communicate their need and who is able to receive and understand that communication. Everything's a circle, everything's interconnected.

Here in *Reckoning X*, Jaime McGhee's "The Over-Sea"—a story about emigrating to the land of the colonizer—denotes speech by indentation, but renders speech *within a colonized mindset* using quotation marks. It's a deliberate, deeply meaningful choice by the author, calling attention to the textual and linguistic violence inherent in a literary medium like this one. Luis Rafael Moya's textual art piece "Agujero Negro" speaks to the same point.

Ten years into making *Reckoning*, I've become we, and we've learned so much. We can see so much more of that interconnectedness than ever before, even as the intersecting crises grow more acute with every year that's passed. And though at times I dread what another ten years might teach me about humanity, where I'd have failed, we keep going.

Reckoning started with a staff of one. After ten years, our editorial staff has included upwards of thirty people from ten countries, speaking eight languages, each of whose lives and minds are completely their own, unlike any other, and each of whom has contributed something indelible to what *Reckoning* has become and is becoming.

We start out not knowing, then we learn from each other. I think that's as good an encapsulation as any of what these past ten years have taught me, about environmental justice, about what it is to be alive, struggling to survive, perceive, communicate, and understand. This issue is packed full of all kinds of different ways of communicating about environmental justice—some soothing, some shocking—from all kinds of different people. Some of it, I very much hope, will blow your mind right open.

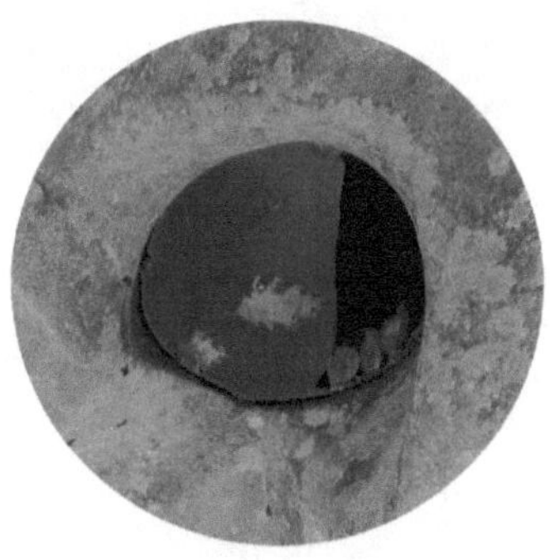

Michael J. DeLuca's short fiction has been appearing since 2005 in markets such as *Beneath Ceaseless Skies*, *Mythic Delirium* and *Apex*. His novella *Night Roll* was a finalist for the Crawford Award in 2020, and his debut novel *The Jaguar Mask* came out from Stelliform Press in August, 2024. He lives in the rapidly suburbifying post-industrial woodlands north of Detroit with wife, kid, cats, plants and microbes. For more, try his website: The Mossy Skull.

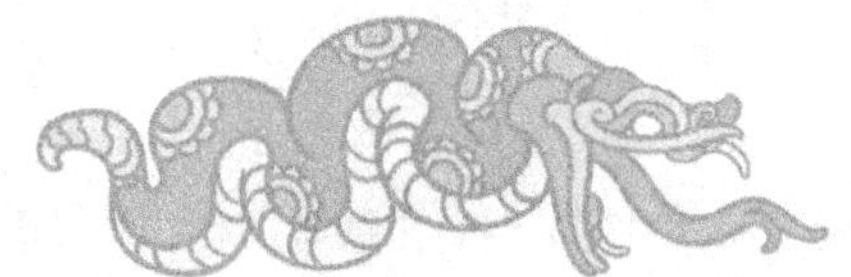

Editorial: **Becoming "We"**

C.G. Aubrey, Priya Chand, Michael J. DeLuca, Ruth Joffre, Hope Joseph, Andrew Kozma, Ellis Nye, Chidera Offor, Catherine Rockwood, and Bernie Jean Schiebeling

[An Exquisite Corpse[1]]

Humans use words. Mushrooms use mycelia. Who's to say which is better? This is why we have infused each copy with spores.

If you're reading this, the psychedelics have already entered your bloodstream. Get ready.

The language of our nervous system, the solar system, any system. We don't hear it? Can you hear the earth burning? The shrieks of languages travailing across species like migrants from another destroyed solar system. The voices of the non-human neighbours pleading to billion deaf ears. Betrayed by alphabets, the language killed by a deficit in the bank of vocabulary. Do you speak/understand the language of the planet?

And if you're not fluent in Disregulated Polysystem, if sometimes these days it seems impossible to believe reason, attention, goodwill, a 'decent ear' should be enough to turn so much noise to signal, well then: what's the strangest living thing you can love and listen to? Stranded between ice and melt, with January sheeted over sidewalks and March shaking the treetops, maybe you think of lichens, moss; if moss, then tardigrades; if tardigrades, then irritated bears who also suffer from unsettled weather. If bears? then skunk cabbage, which heats itself inside a fruitful mire. Red-hulled stinking food. Saying in its own way, come here—come soon.

Listening gathers silence and casts light into the countless corners of an ever-connecting web. We coalesce at the intersections like

1. Exquisite Corpse is a storytelling game, invented by French Surrealists in the 1920s, wherein each participant adds a single line after having seen only the previous line. The title refers to a line from one of the game's first incarnations: "Le cadavre exquis boira le vin nouveau." ("The exquisite corpse shall drink the new wine.")

dew drops, each our own glimmer until we all become a single shine. Until we are all water and sunlight and rainbow refractions, myriad reflections we only sometimes believe.

Below us, we know, is a darkness we cannot fathom, a hollow our refractions cannot touch. But it's always been there.

The rain ends and the worms squirm forth, singing. Like orpiment wine, the sun spills across the field; the tender brush unfurl to tap into the light, decussate leaves bobbing up eastward. This is the force of change. No one gets what they want—except us, and we want a happy ending.

So go, sip at the new sun. Listen for what you've always missed. Thousands of years ago, human hands traced ochred animals along Chauvet's stone, painting the slope of a snout, the hunch of shoulders. Let your fingertips sink into warm clay, and know that it is not too late to begin again.

Editorial: **Everything's Environmental Justice**

C.G. Aubrey

As Michael says, "Everything is environmental justice", and well "everything" is a lot, but it's also true. Take fair elections. They may not seem at first glance to be connected to environmental justice, but in places without fair and equal representation, those who stand to suffer the most have the least power to protect themselves from environmental injustices like climate change vulnerabilities, pollution, and displacement.

In red-lined and gerrymandered states across the US, privileged political and economic elites vote against clean energy and line their pockets with money from oil and coal lobbyists, but coal ash doesn't wind up in *their* water supplies. They invite and encourage pollution hotspots like data centers, power plants, and refineries to build or dump in poor, rural, disproportionately racialized communities with willful disregard for the health and welfare of the people, the surrounding land, and the water supply. Because dumping—both literal and metaphorical—always occurs downstream.

We've seen this kind of inequality before in places like Flint, Michigan, where it's been twenty years and the primarily Black community is still only beginning to see justice. We see it continuing in climate-vulnerable communities, especially along the coasts where rising sea levels threaten those who can't afford to leave. We see it across Appalachia, where mountain top removal mining contaminates water and air and creates ever worsening health crises. Now, maybe more than ever, we need free elections. To move the scales towards justice everyone must have a voice, and those voices must be represented equally.

In this way, environmental justice is connected to gender equality, to disability rights, to fair lending practices, to immigration and labor laws, to education, and communication. The list is endless because, ultimately, environmental justice challenges unequal and failing systems; it demands new ways of thinking, of communicating, of being.

Environmental justice reminds us, more than anything, that we are all (and always) connected. I hope the works collected here in our beautiful tenth issue show how much those connections matter.

Thanks to all of you for an amazing decade.

C.G. Aubrey is a queer, AuDHD writer and outdoor enthusiast obsessed with yellow leaves, swamp rainbows, and em dashes. She holds dual-masters degrees in US History and Religious Studies and often finds inspiration at the intersection of cultural memory, religion, and the environment. Her story "A Predatory Transience" appeared in Reckoning in 2023; she's been editing here ever since. Find her occasionally on Bluesky @cgaubrey.bsky.social, Instagram @c.g.aubrey, and www.cgaubrey.com.

Antediluvian

Rem Wigmore

Your house isn't flooded in the conventional sense. It's an unconventional flood.

You knew about the rising seas and that, but this was faster, like the kind of disaster movie that pisses off your mates who work at MetService. One day it was the usual Wellington, can't beat it, mushrooms in the cupboard, then the next day, with no tsunami and no warning, came the flood.

It's a deep, calming, unlikely flood—no sewage in the water, fish and eels and dolphins all swimming by. You're better off than the people who get really fucked over when there's floods, but it's hard to look on the bright side.

The news broadcast says not to use any motorboats when getting around the city so you don't scare the cetaceans, whales and dolphins and orca. You really feel you're more scared of orca than they are of you. When you see them, you climb to the roof, toss pebbles into the still waters, and watch them sink into the impossibly clear depths.

The roof of your building used to just be where you huddled to vape before you quit, and now it reminds you of cliff diving with your cousins out in the bay. But less rocks, more concrete. Clear water, scary deep, the footpath on one side with the canal the road's turned into, and the tiny, drowned courtyard on the other. Only the fish can party there now. Occasionally a purloined traffic cone bobs fluorescently past, borne by unknown currents to unknown seas.

Because this definitely isn't cold enough to be the Pacific. And it's fresh water, which makes it even more confusing, and also it's not like you're about to drink it, so what a waste. You wave down the Delivereasy driver when they row past with Powerade.

What can you do? You batten the hatches. You call in sick to work, because all your clothes are soaked, and the laundromat is underwater.

Kev down the road says the owners fished some of the washing machines out with bungy hooks, and that they're renting them out as waterproof lockers. The world turned on its head, rotated on spin cycle.

Your poet friend Minerva tells you the flood's a metaphor, and you say yeah, I know that, mate, but knowing doesn't stop the mould on all my clothes, soggy shoes and nothing to wear to work today.

On a call with your parents you tell them you're getting by. On a zoom call with your ex you tell them you're doing great. In a voice chat with your mates, too late at night, you say maybe it's time to make your peace with the flood; floods can bring beautiful things too. Silt. Change. Ducks.

The next day you get a text that you're fired.

You can't be the only person to call in flooded. You post on the message boards about workers' rights, and the mods delete it as a joke, because no one can ever believe anything bad happens in New Zealand. The Citizens' Advice Bureau is underwater, your union rep doesn't pick up, Fair Go stopped years ago. What can you do?

When your union rep finally gets back to you they can't help, because all your paperwork was filed under your old name and gender and you break the systems, and they don't say it out loud, but their voice is . . . kind of sus. Like they think you being trans brought on the flood, like you're fucking Moses, or Noah or whoever, but you feel more like that guy who woke up as a beetle, except you don't even get to be famous *or* a beetle.

Fuck your boss, anyway.

You hold your breath and dive back into your apartment. Battle through all the floating hoodies and business-casual fits and those sparkly shorts from when you went to Ivy, and you fetch the pufferfish who lives in your room, because from the roof you still get signal, you know where your boss lives, and you're going to straight up fugu a motherfucker—

Because violence is bad, right, but you're cold and drenched and you can't live like this, you're not Aquaman. And you can't get back at every asshole who landed you here, but you can get back at *Name Redacted*, who is on the rich list, who lives uphill, and who voted for the party that put through the Floodwater Everywhere And Lots Of It Bill.

You bribe a passing kayaker with your last packet of instant noodles, and you're underway.

It's a long trip. The wind picks up, and you wish you'd traded a keep cup or something for a life jacket. Choppy waves splash at the bow.

Even when you get there, you stay in the kayak for a hot minute, bobbing against the walls of his house. "We can do this," you tell the pufferfish, like it's gonna either encourage or stop you, but it's a fish. It has a sweet little face, though. Doesn't look scared, even though you're keeping it in a laundry basket. It's not even puffering. The wind is cold.

If you don't like getting flooded, fish probably don't like getting laundry basketed.

You hold the basket under the waves and watch the little guy swim free. Something of yourself leaves with it, and you feel lighter. Like you've let go of something, like you can breathe easier. Like . . . you came from water, too, and maybe it's not so bad to go back.

Then you find a marker that still works, and you write on your boss's wall—what used to be the second storey of his house on the hill, and is now the ground floor—

Fuck you man

but that doesn't really cover it, so you add,

Justice to those who bring the flood

because you think it sounds good, and underneath you write,

This is not a metaphor.

And you row back. Along the way a blue penguin pops up from the water beside you and inspects you for a second, as if it has that same fellow-feeling, cousins living the life aquatic. Then it dives again, leaving a sense of wonder and a strong stench of fish. The sun shines bright and blue on the submerged capital. The wind isn't too bad really, but you wonder if anyone's thought of using sails here.

Rowing is pretty fun.

Maybe you'll be a dinghy food-deliverer, bringing people bread and milk and firewood. Row past the killer whales with a kind of 'you don't bother me, I won't bother you' policy.

For now, you move to your roof. That night your mates come by with a shitty Kmart tent and you play cards, like you're just camping, and life feels like real life again. Go fish.

Rem Wigmore is a speculative fiction writer from Aotearoa New Zealand, author of the Vengeful Wild duology (*Foxhunt* and *Wolfpack*). Rem's other works include *Riverwitch* and *The Wind City*. Their short fiction is published in venues including *Baffling Magazine*, *Worlds of Possibility* and two *Year's Best Aotearoa New Zealand Science Fiction & Fantasy* anthologies. In 2023, Rem won the Sir Julius Vogel Award for Best Fan Writing with their climate fiction essay 'Conservation, Red in Tooth and Claw'. Rem's probably a changeling, but you're stuck with them now. The coffee here is just too good. Rem can be found online at remwigmore.com.

Newspaper Erasures as Questions with Answers for Two Cities

Sneha Subramanian Kanta

I.

[Is   Coastal Road worth   ecology?]

we must speak about the land as an orbit an erosion
a map carbonized into the helm of cinderblocks
you are playing with Mumbai like we play a game of cards

[may decongest the city. But   people   places it will harm?]

in a physics class I kept hearing *plants*
when my teacher said *planks*

[at a time when fisherfolk, like other   communities,   struggling to recover   the heavy blow of the   pandemic.
"Had you been there   you would have had tears
     ,"   . "I invite   come live with us for two days,
          .   not even have vegetables   with *rotis* sometimes."]

the truest sentence is a hailstone.
because the Arabian sea is swallowing our city
where it is being built for wealth regardless of tides
where tomorrow's ancestors are today's elusive parents.
my father walked barefoot to a temple several times
to pray to a goddess, this temple is situated upon the Arabian sea
where now my mother's ashes are mixed with water
in the pandemic in a new country, we move ten houses
in twelve months. our cartilages remember a country
as sponging throbs of firmament emptying into rain

[, an assistant professor
                                        calls this a "skewed idea of planning".]

tell me the history which will not be written in books
and I will tell you the cleaving of a family, how it begins

["Our beaches will go underwater, currents will change,
shoreline eroding faster, loss of biodiversity,
livelihood of fishermen destroyed. an exercise in
extravaganza could have been avoided,
," . "This belief restore nature
from every mind,]

my mother's father was a fisherman, a Koli
with significant ties to water. we all will be connected
to water is a story which will yield a life.
the water turned alkaline, nana, before I could
leave the country. the word for alkaline in Marathi
is अल्कधर्मी. when calling out to God, I weep in Marathi.

II.

['100-year-storm' batters Mississauga, damage could have
been worse]

when it rains, rasped, thunderstorm blur knots
churning the city into water into lake into pond into river
ocular and abject, I remember the Credit River for its amplitudes
of sound, cultivating entire forest marshlands
why are you thinking about wealth with the alliteration of water?

[While storms like the one are rare–the last comparable
in 2013–experts say climate change could trigger more
temperatures climbing just one
degree .]

for two years, the cherry trees have begun to bloom
earlier due to rising temperatures. a congregation of families
will arrive to watch the eighty trees at Kariya Park.
two cities are called sisters. after refrains of fog bridled
into the balconies of high rises, eyelids will sketch pestles

of autumn leaves that surpass an erosive winter.
when I leave a country, the birds meet me in sutures of cities.

[, the stormwater drainage system more than 51,000 catchbasins, 270 kilometres ditches, 150 kilometres creeks, 81 stormwater management facilities (including ponds, ,) that help collect, drain, and clean rainwater runoff before it enters Lake Ontario, the source of drinking water.]

Two 100-year storms hit our city in a month.
A distillation prayer of an immigrant passes through
widening trees into the greenbelt, exiting the city as the Credit River
takes new forms. With the city changes the country
and then the world. Except water, in its memory
of taking form through rituals against slants of cartography.
I won't say I have left the Arabian Sea of changing waters.
In his last years, my paati's anna kept calling God in Tamil.
When I was a girl in a sprawling temple of gingelly oil lamps
I asked my mother if God will understand my prayers in English.
God understands all languages, my mother would say.
Now I pray in malls, parking lots, bus stops, empty rooms.
Through water, I step out of the borders of a country.
If we won't listen, will water—

will water take formless thuds; throb, ferried into everything,
as if a country as if an unmooring, liquefying into an auspicate
inexhaustible source of oneness?

Sneha Subramanian Kanta is the author of the chapbooks *Ghost Tracks* (Louisiana Literature Press, 2020), *Ancestral–Wing* (Porkbelly Press, forthcoming), and *Every Elegy Is A Love Poem* (Variant Lit, forthcoming). She is a recipient of the 2022 Digital Residency from The Seventh Wave and the 2021 Robert Hayden Scholarship at Stockton University. She is the recipient of the inaugural Vijay Nambisan Fellowship 2019. She is the Charles Wallace Fellow writer in residence (2019-20) at The University of Stirling. Most recently, her poem won the Canadian Authors Association—Toronto inaugural Poetry Prize 2022. Her multi-genre work is forthcoming in *Prairie Schooner*, *Geist*, Sheridan's *The Ampersand Review*, and elsewhere. Website: www.snehasubramaniankanta.com

Photo by Sushant Hembrom. unsplash.com/@susmac007

The Over-Sea

Jamie McGhee

On the island, there is too much blood and not enough rain. That's because the wetleaf is gone. The soldiers told us to kill it: to slice and strangle the emerald vines as they flowed over our hills, those rivulets of paradise, seafoam soft. So we sliced and we strangled and we killed. And now we cradle the wetleaf in our palms, sitting with each plant as it dies.

The soldiers pry the wetleaf from our mourning fingers and command us to replace it with something better. Indigo, they say. Grow indigo for the mainland, for de metropool.

But without the wetleaf roots, the soil can't hold; it lets go of its water, releasing it to evaporate into the sky and seep back into sea, and when the water goes, the indigo withers, and when we surrender piles of mangled indigo leaves at the boots of the soldiers—*sir, there's nothing we can do*—they turn their rifles and they aim at us.

~

I recoil from my reflection in the steel of their guns. My eyes are bloated yellow moons in a flat black face, terror refracted back unto itself.

~

One day, in the searing summer swelt, two soldiers drag a sobbing farmer behind a packing-barn and grind his nose into the soil. They harvest bullets out of an ammo pouch and plant one in the back of his neck—in the juncture where the occipital bone meets the atlas, I will later learn—soaking the earth with his own red water. The metropool's emblem glints in Dutch orange and cobalt blue as the trigger draws back again. When blood splatters, it looks like flecks of misplaced rain.

The next month, another farmer. Then a teacher. Then a boy. I stumble over a friend of a friend, and discover a colony of fly eggs ripening in his dead, swelling flesh.

~

The soldiers are homesick. They tell us that. They look earnest when they ask why we are making their lives so hard. As they talk, flies weave and wobble near their open mouths as if they might swim inside to find shade from the heat.

Okay,

I say.

I am the first to learn their language. Ja, meneer. Nee, meneer. Yes, sir. No. Instead of naming plants, I say gewassen and winsten, crops and profits.

We tear out more plants to make room for more profits.

~

Grab the wetleaf by the stomach, by the root, by the throat. Twist.

~

I am eleven when I hear her dying. My classmate. She groans beneath my kitchen window, body contorted into a heaving, panting tumbleweed, a tangle of blood and limbs. She groans for her mother. She groans for her mother, and she moves her arms as if to crawl, but she goes nowhere.

I witness her, vinegar bile crawling up my throat and into my mouth. I'm trying not to faint. I tell myself,

Do something.

Can I overpower the soldier for his rifle? Can I scream loud enough on the island for the mainland to hear?

I tear my sleeping shirt into a bandage and run with arms extended to carry her. My sister holds me back in the doorway.

She says,

Don't touch her.

I say—

But my sister stops me again.

She says,

That bullet is lodged in the girl's spine.

She means,

Touching the girl will only break her more.

She means,

If a soldier sees you, you'll join her.

My mother runs for the girl's family. My brother calls for the priest.

I am the only one who doesn't understand, foolish enough to think we can still piece her back together. I ask,

How do we get the bullet out?

as if it were so simple.

My sister fixes her mouth into a grim line, a pressed and unsmiling stripe of flesh.

Doctors live on our island, but those doctors are not for us. We used to have our own doctors: bonesetters and soothers who could distill wetleaf into salves and balms, who could turn its seeds into a healing thing, who prayed to the earth as they foraged its clovers and passed those blessings onto the people they touched.

But our bonesetters uprooted themselves when the soldiers arrived. They dug themselves out and took to the winds, scattered themselves to the other islands that still had wetleaf hills.

The doctors who live on our island now live over the mountain, where you need a car to go.

They live by the signatuurleer, the doctrine of signatures. Their white hands only treat white bodies.

When I worry,

So who will treat the girl?

the question is too large and misshapen to fit all the way inside my mouth.

Outside and beneath the window, the girl curls into her final knotted form. Her parents arrive just in time to watch her spirit leave, soaking back into the earth. A soldier tries and fails to keep them five paces away from her. They run forward. The soldier fumbles for his ammo pouch again.

A different question works its way out of my throat:
And those white hands—
where did they learn their medicine?
Wherever the white doctors came from, I will go there.

When I finish school, my family pools their savings, and it is not enough. And my mother sells her jewelry, and it is not enough. And the entire island collects money, and it is not enough, not nearly enough. And I sign myself over to the metropolitan colonial bank for a loan that is more than my family has seen across three generations, and when I am terrified and the ink is dry and my body is no longer my own, the university bursar says that it will do.

"The metropool produces all doctors because the metropool produces all knowledge. In the metropool, knowledge is free and fair, balanced and polite, given to all who ask."

How do I know? Because a professor says so. She stands at the front of the lecture hall and assures us that this is true.

It is my first day at the medisch instituut van de metropool. I nod and nod. I write this down. I do not have time to think about whether I believe it. It does not matter whether I believe it. I bury it deep in the furrows of my brain, to root out later, on the test.

My sister packed me ginger yucca, dried into long salted stripes. I eat them slowly, letting each crumb dissolve down into nothing before I swallow, disappear slowly down the creeks of my throat. I will try to make a week's worth of home last all six years.

~

The island and the metropool have spoken the same language since the soldiers came, but in the metropool, they insist I am speaking it wrong.

A lecturer halts my first oral exam. "Stop. Just—stop."

He rubs his forehead and he waves me out of the room. I stand, and I wait, and I wait before I leave, as if he might change his mind. He doesn't. My shoulders stoop under a sudden weight, but I drag myself into the hallway and manage to stay standing. I tell myself,

It's okay.

I will try harder. I am in classes eight hours a day, and working eight hours a day, and studying eight hours a day, but I will find a magical twenty-fifth hour, and I will use it to practice speech in the mirror, practice working my tongue around the same words I've been saying since childhood, but this time in a new direction.

~

As I leave the examination hall, the student-assistent catches my arm. Her nails are coral crescent moons and she squeezes sympathy into the crook of my elbow.

She says, "What they're doing to you is unfair."

She says, "It's violent and it's not right."

I think she means the exam, but then she mentions tobacco and colonies, soldiers and children. She says that she will fight for us.

I nod, wondering if this student-assistent—this fighter—is grading our conversation.

So when I say,

Dank u wel,

I try to scrub the words free of my accent before handing them over.

~

The night before I left, my sister shook me awake.

She did not say,

Good luck,

or,

I will miss you.

Instead, she wrapped me in a tight and tendriled hug, refusing to let go:

If you need to come home, just find the ocean. Please remember how to swim.

Instead, I drown. My list of failures grows. After Academische Vorming it is Scheikunde; it is Organische Chemie, Klinische Methodologie, Structurele Biologie. The lecturers tell me,

You should have mastered this material already.

One laughs about the island, attempting a joke about our magic flowers.

I want to tell them,

When I was a child, before the soldiers, I dug my knowledge out of the earth. If you give me a molecule I can crack it open in my hands like a pomegranate; I can point out all its pieces and show you how they vibrate inside seeds and stems. Why do you keep asking me to write it down? Can't you feel the vibrations too?

I want to tell them this, but I don't. I just study harder. I start to sleep in the university library, tucking my arms into myself as if I'm folding in my leaves.

One night, the fighter shakes my shoulder. "You're not allowed to sleep here."

My eyes ache as I repack my bag. But instead of kicking me out, the fighter passes a thermos of tea beneath my nose, white steam climbing up the air like vines, and she smiles at the shock on my face when I smell it. Wetleaf. Where did she get—

"I bought my own plant a few years ago," she says. Hesitates. Lowers her eyes. "But now it's a bit sick."

Dried tendrils break off in my fist.

Exhausted leaves, stretching for a certain sunlight they will never find here, so far from home.

As the fighter watches, I cradle the wetleaf pot and shift it to her western window, in the direction of the ocean.

People are talking about liberation.

Who?

I bark into the receiver. The call costs three guilder a minute, but I have to know.

Who's talking about treason?

My sister says,

Just people.

I clutch her through the payphone.

Don't go near people like that.

Do you think I'm crazy? Of course I won't.

Listen to me.

Why are you yelling?

Because people like that get executed. People like that get shot in the back of the head—

In the juncture where the occipital bone meets the atlas, waar het os occipitale het atlas ontmoet. I know those words now.

No,

says my sister.

They get shot in the chest now.

What?

The soldiers like to see their eyes.

As she speaks, she pulls away. I feel it through the phone. Her voice dims, and she becomes a ganzania flower curling away its petals, retreating into the dark.

But,

she says softly, further away,

sometimes people survive getting shot in the chest. It's not the spine. Sometimes people survive.

While I am resitting the failed exams, the loan runs dry. I have to stop studying so that I can work. Because I have to stop studying, the metropool takes my visa. The university alerts immigration as soon as I don't register for classes, and a letter arrives in the mail, grim black lettering on despondent dead trees. They give me seven days.

All I can do is drag out my suitcase and open it. I hug my knees and stare down into the empty, beaten plastic.

I make a call.

The fighter lets herself into my apartment. She sits on the edge of my bed. I take her hand and she knots her fingers around mine, tangling our roots.

We cannot get married in the metropool. There's too much paperwork, too many regulations; the metropool knows its citizens marry not for love but for guilt, marry the unwanted people the metropool built brick borders to keep out. So we take a ferry to the next country east, which promises fast ceremonies and few questions.

I pay for the marriage license, and I pay the visa application fee, and I pay the visa processing fee, and I work under the table in the village of Løgumkloster, tending shrubs for a church that takes pity while we wait for the approval, and when the paperwork gets lost I pay it all again. And in between, I study. And the fighter and I cook chervil soup with the herbs that we forage from the consecrated soil.

The marriage certificate is a foreign object in my fists. If I ever thought I would be married, it was never like this. When the fighter smiles at me, I smile back wider, vinehooks stretching up the corners of my mouth.

After eight weeks, we are allowed to return to the metropool. At the border, a hundred people form two lines inside an airless white room.

One soldier drains his water bottle and tugs at the soaked cotton of his shirt, surveying the onslaught of sweaty black skin. “It’s a jungle in here.”

I think he means the heat. The fighter insists he means the people. She snaps at him before I can beg her to wait.

No!

I say.

She didn’t mean—

Soldiers confiscate our bags. Inspection, they claim, and empty my rucksack onto the floor. A Dutch Shepherd sniffs my books, her clothes, my books again.

The lock us in a room without windows. Sterile in its lack of oxygen.

I surrender my head onto my crossed arms on the table. The hot day exhales long into night as thirst crusts along my tongue. I remind myself that the fighter will always fight.

They return our passports at sunrise. By then, there is another fight.

The entire island is under attack.

I press my face to the hissing television screen. Soldiers storm across the island, spraying alien clouds of toxic gas. Crops lie mangled and half-formed in ravaged fields, torn up like naked corpses robbed from their graves. The sky bends and seethes overhead. In the trees, there are snipers where there should be birds. More gas unfurls in Dutch orange and cobalt blue. A cancerous yellow dust descends onto plants and outstretched palms.

Pesticide spray hits the camera lens. I taste it on my teeth. I swallow hard, and even though I am an ocean away, the gas finds my lips and blisters its way down.

My sister doesn’t pick up the phone.

I call again. I call again.

The silence that grows between us is large enough to fit bodies in.

❧

I press a hand to the leaded television glass as if I could grab the soldiers by stomach, by the root, by the throat.

❧

I call again.

❧

The fighter and I buy a newspaper for the journey home. Berooking. That is the word the metropool selects to describe what they're doing: de berooking, covering the island in smoke. In foreign papers, they translate it exsufflation.

Berooking is an old word, a lost word, a blank word that conjures up no pictures. It is a word no one has used in a hundred years and a word that no one understands now. So it is a word no one can oppose. It is perfect for the metropool.

I look up a better translation. Fumigation.

They claim they are chasing off pests.

❧

"We have to do something," the fighter tells me.

I unlock the apartment for the first time in eight weeks. I set down our suitcases. I linger over the metal clasps and think of everything but my sister, but the smoke.

Fumigation.

The fighter craters her fist into her palm. "We have a duty to protest," she says, because she has been waiting for this moment. "We have a duty to stop this."

A duty. I seal our marriage certificate into a heavy envelope.

I unload the bills from the mailbox and stack university enrollment forms on the table. My fingers are a violent tremor and I curl them into the safety of fists until they stop shaking. I remind myself of why I am here, and the people who need me to study until I become useful. This room smells stale with dust and I've already wasted too much time.

I have other duties,

I say. I spread a hand across the papers.

I have other duties first.

Why does it sound like an apology?

Why does she look at me in disappointment?

That night, to pay for it all, I scrub tiles. And the night after that, and the night after that. I scour linoleum on my hands and knees in the universitair psychiatrisch centrum for six guilders an hour, scraping away black dirt tracked in by white shoes. In the metropool, knowledge is freely given, so I'm given the knowledge of how to remove mildew with sodium hypochlorite.

When the fumes leave me dizzy, I drop the mop too freely back into the bucket; industrial bleach splashes out, hits my arms, and burns, and burns, and I imagine my family on the island and feel them burning too.

I sprint to the payphone before I'm allowed a break. A coworker advances me a guilder, and this time, my sister picks up on the second ring.

Hey.

From seven thousand kilometers away, I plant kisses in the angry ridges of her frowning forehead. I plant them like neat little rows of indigo.

Between shifts, I study for the courses I will have to retake. The medisch instituut van de metropool rejects my re-enrollment, but I tell myself another school will accept me. Some school, somewhere, if I just learn how to learn. So I practice flattening organisms onto paper, practice labeling them, practice seeing humans as diagrams and not living things.

One morning, the fighter snaps my textbook shut. "I'm protesting the berooking in front of parliament." She grips the table. "Come with me."

I tell her,

Maybe when I'm done.

But I know that I shouldn't.

Yet by nightfall, the guilt sets in. I leave my second shift the minute it's over and follow a stream of protestors to the plein-square outside parliament. Police have blocked and barricaded every entrance, cutting off the tributary streets pooling people inward. Police dogs snarl, twisting on the leash. I stand one block away to refuse them my scent.

I cannot see the protest but I can hear it: the crack of police batons, the pop of fists, the brief spray of water from a canon. Later, breathless and pansy-pink with adrenaline, the fighter will show me photographs of dislodged teeth scattered like white flower petals in pools of red.

I did not think that violence could ever breach *this* side of the ocean. I realize that perhaps it started here.

One week later, police find my front door. They bang.

I freeze at the kitchen table. They scream a word I don't know and threaten to tear the whole wall down. When I don't respond, they scream louder. The word is a name.

I open the door.

That name isn't mine.

They barge inside anyway, mud on their boots. "Your neighbors swear he lives here."

But that name is not even from my island. That name is from another hemisphere, occupied on the other side of the world; the metropool has tentacles in every ocean.

Those tentacles are why they chose my island to fumigate first. *People are talking about liberation.* We'd fallen out of line. Now the metropool has made us the example. We earn them no money anyway, because on my island there is blood but no rain and no indigo. Being the example is what we are good for.

This is both the history and the truth, but police care about neither. One photographs my passport. The other searches the corners of my apartment. Clipped to their hips, nine-millimeter pistols catch the light. I retreat behind the counter and knuckle it discreetly, remembering the girl and the soldiers, thinking of all the soft parts of my body the officers could shoot me in.

What did the man do?

I ask.

The woman makes sharp eye contact. "He's being charged with oproer."

Oproer. The word is familiar but I look it up again once they leave. Uproar. They mean that he was dark and foreign at a protest. They mean that he left his apartment wearing the wrong shade of skin.

"Police are just trying to scare you," the fighter says. "Come to the protest this time. Cover your face and you'll be fine."

But I need her to understand:

It's not that simple.

The night that the police finally track down the man, a pile of trash appears outside the apartment block. No, not trash. His belongings. Tank tops and spectacles. A box of old magazines, a handful of loose and boardless chess pieces, a potted hibiscus. And a law textbook. I wonder who on his island was counting on him here.

I rescue the hibiscus when it starts to rain. Only when it sits inside on my shelf, contained beside the dying wetleaf, both plants facing the window and watching the fresh water wash down, do I wonder whether it may have preferred to stay outside.

That same night, the fighter stays outside too. Four a.m, five a.m., six a.m., and she still is not home. By the time she stumbles in after sunrise, I'm getting ready for work.

I ask her where she was. I promise myself that I don't mind. I just want to know where. I want to know who.

She met a man at the protest. She calls him her new friend. "We painted something near the parliament building," she says, proud. "You'll see it on the news."

I tell her I've stopped following local news.

The downward slit of her mouth tells me this was the wrong answer. She sits. Fidgets. "You know, *he's* from your island too, but he's protesting anyway."

She wants me to feel impressed, I think, or guilty. Instead, I ask,

Oh? Which side of the mountain?

I could just as well ask:

What color are his parents' hands?

She recoils. "I meant, his father is from the island."

I ask,

So your new friend grew up *here*?

She says, "He did."

I ask,

He's a citizen *here*?

She says, "He is."

I say,

So it's different.

Silence ripens and then spoils in the air between us. I say again,

It's different. Isn't it?

She is quiet. Shifts. "I guess it could be."

She folds her palm over mine, smothering my skin in her shadows. Her body blocks the sunlight that was just starting to reach me through the window.

Later, I sit with an immigration officer.

If my wife is arrested, I won't get deported, will I?

I will be able to keep studying?

He says, "It's not that simple."

The medisch instituut van de metropool rejects my final appeal, but the institut médical de la métropole invites me to an entrance exam, one country over. When the invitation letter arrives, giddiness and terror split my heart in equal measure. It has to be different this time.

I tell the fighter I'll be gone for a week. After a stiff hug, she asks if she can open our apartment to her friends while I'm gone, asks if other protestors can use it as a den. If people can come over. If people can spend the night.

I'd rather you didn't,

I say.

But when I return, I find a belt under the bed. It's not my belt. I stare at it. I am dizzy. Then I strip the sheets. And I lie on the mattress and look up at the ceiling and I imagine her new friend rolling all over my bed, grunting, sweating, rutting, snarling like a brute, howling like a monkey, the way they say all people from my island are apes, are creatures, are senseless and barking sacks of blackened flesh.

The soldiers claim they have successfully exsufflated every field on the island. That means the crops are dead or dying. When desperate people scrounge in the dirt for irradiated scraps, the soldiers spray them like weeds, first with gas, then with bullets, claiming it's for their own protection.

I beg my sister not to risk foraging in the hills. I say,

Stay inside.

She says,

And eat what?

I swear to her that I will figure something out. But horror builds in the base of my throat and I can't choke it down. When I eat, I throw up, as if that will do them any good.

At the kitchen table, I am sitting and staring into an empty bowl when the fighter comes home, a newspaper crooked beneath her arm. She's been gone for three days.

She slides it to me. I slide it back. I don't need pictures to understand that they are starving.

She asks, "How can you study like nothing has changed? Doesn't it bother you at all?"

I pause. What is there to say? I extend my hand and she cups her cheek into it, kisses my wrist. Her mouth is a foreign thing. I pull away.

How do I explain that I have to study *because* nothing has changed?

❧

In her sleep, the fighter groans. She groans, and she moves her arms as if to crawl, but she goes nowhere. Perhaps, in her dreams, she meets my classmate.

❧

My mother needs money but doesn't know how to ask. I feel it in the pauses between her words. But I am confused, because I've been wiring money to my sister for months.

My mother goes quiet.

That means:

My family needs a lot of it all at once.

That means:

It's an emergency.

I sway on my feet. I don't want to know, but I need to know. Somehow, I find the question and force it out:

Who?

Another pause, and I know it was my sister.

She was foraging for wetleaf and—

❧

I take a third job cleaning at another hospital. When a letter from the institut médical de la métropole arrives, a fat letter, a congratulations, I glance inside and I toss it into a box. I let it lie fallow beside a growing stack of bills. I need to send more money home. Medical school can wait, has to wait, always has to wait one more semester.

Besides, the island has doctors now.

Doctors, now.

On the island, the metropool has set up a humanitarian clinic for the people that they gassed. They made sure it made big headlines in big newspapers because it makes the metropool look good. Benevolent. Like a bougainvillea flower that blooms into such a violent and vibrant shade of magenta that its petals distract from its thorns.

Inside the clinic, my sister is still alive, but only just. And the clinic charges by the day.

The fighter has started sleeping at home again, instead of disappearing every night. She is careful never to notice me out loud: she doesn't mention my closed medical textbooks gathering dust, or my clothes smelling like industrial bleach, or my first streaks of grey sprouting at one temple.

One evening, she sits down. And I sit down. And I realize we have nothing to talk about.

"I'm hunger-striking in solidarity," she says finally. She peels open her lips and rot curls out. She tells me that is how hunger smells, the body dissolving itself.

But no one else is striking. Since the clinic opened, people have stopped caring about the island. They think the problem is solved.

She explains this now as if I do not know. And I let her, because at least it isn't silence. If she ever asks me, I will tell her about the seafoam softness of our hills and how it felt to kill the vines.

She pauses to wince. "Hey, can you help me with—"

When she lifts one pant leg, blood seeps shyly from a cut along her calf. It's deeper than the cuts that came before. By now, she knows the policemen by name. She could point out the one who did this, but it wouldn't make a difference. She sighs. It is a different pain than mine, but I recognize that we sigh on the same frequency.

I open the first aid kit. It's almost empty, so I dab the wound with alcohol and study it, trying to decide what to do. Finally, I fetch the potted wetleaf. It has been sickly for years, but sickly is not dead. The hibiscus is long dead. But the wetleaf, somehow, is still thrumming. I stroke a few leaves and before I pluck them, I thank the plant for sharing itself with me.

I work the leaves into a mortar and pestle with two drops of sunflower oil and a pinch of salt: the oil to sooth, the salt to disinfect, the wetleaf to draw the skin back together. For the first time in a long time, my hands work without thinking. Soon they smell like my sister's hands did when I was a child, a little like lemon, a little like mint, when she'd layer wetleaf into bandages over my scraped knees. She told me my mother had once done the same for her. Perhaps my sister should be here studying medicine instead of me. Or perhaps I should be there studying plants. I drop a fistful of withered petals into a mug and let them steep.

I kneel to paint the poultice onto the fighter's wound. She jerks away in pain, hissing. She says, "Are you sure that—"

I press the mug of tea into her hands. White steam climbs up the air like vines. It has been so long since we drank this together. Her face settles into something like serenity. Something like, but not quite. Serenity requires a certain sunlight that doesn't exist on this side of the sea.

I finish wrapping her leg. She lets me work. Then I go to my room. I open my suitcase, close it. Open my rucksack instead. In the end, I take only my passport, and break off more three small leaves from the plant.

"Where are you going?" The fighter stops me at the door. "When will you be back?"

I shade my eyes and blink out toward the evening sun. It's starting to dip in the direction I want to walk. And I don't know if I'll make it, but I know I want to go; I know I need to swallow a fistful of the sea. So I step into the light and say,

To the ocean.

Jamie McGhee is a Caribbean novelist and historian. Her books include *You Mean It or You Don't: James Baldwin's Radical Challenge* (with Dr. Hollowell of Duke University) and *What I Must Tell the World: The Story of Lorraine Hansberry* (with director Lena Waithe). McGhee's work has been supported by Harvard University, MIT, Zurich University of the Arts and Instituto Sacatar. More information is available at www.Jamie-McGhee.com.

10, 000 Caverns

Elinor Ann Walker

My neighbor through the woods
has cemented over half his yard
near the culvert, built brick walls
where white oak trees used to be.
I'm not sure what he was thinking.
Proud of his trail cam, he says
he's a hunter, knows the land.
He hasn't lived in Tennessee
that long, the state with more
caves than any other. Ground
water seeps up to ephemeral
streams along woodland edges,
finds the lowest point, and I hope
it always will. I don't tell him this
(he can't hear anyway, deafened
by leaf blower, chain saw, power
washer). Outside to get a signal,
he shouts into his cell phone
as I imagine the pull from below,
what might sink, yield drop by drop
to limestone, mineral deposits,
stalactites reach to stalagmites
sturdy enough to lean on, pillars
circling dark lakes where pale,
blind fish drift. But water recedes
in drought even underground;
Lost Sea lost sea, 25 feet, then
recovered. So he probably won't
notice until there's a real flood.
I doubt he'll float by on his boat
to save us. The state of things now.
My boots suck through the thaw
as I slog back to the house. In April,
what remains of my tracks will glisten
with tadpoles if heavy rains still come.

Note: Lost Sea, a real place near Sweetwater, TN, is a large underground lake in the Craighead Caverns cave system.

Elinor Ann Walker is the author of *Fugitive but Gorgeous*, winner of the 2024 Sheila-Na-Gig First Chap Prize (Sheila-Na-Gig Editions), and *Give Sorrow* (Whittle Micro-Press), both forthcoming. Her poetry appears or is forthcoming in many journals, including *AGNI*, *American Poetry Journal*, *Nimrod International Journal*, *Plant-Human Quarterly*, *Plume*, *Poet Lore*, *Quarterly West*, *The Southern Review*, and *Terrain*. She holds a Ph.D. in English from the UNC-Chapel Hill, lives in the Appalachian foothills, and is on the poetry staff of *River Heron Review*. Find her online: https://elinorannwalker.com

The Eternal Hourglass

Kevin J. Binder

I meet Tara once and only once, on my last trip to Rose Isle, two days before Hurricane Zeta hits. The Category 4 storm is still spinning somewhere beyond the southern horizon, hundreds of miles offshore, as my crew and I reach the bridge from the mainland. Out the windshield, I can see the occasional cloud pushing past, and if I try hard enough, I can convince myself that each one's isolated, with no connection to the others.

We're crammed three to a cab in our F-650, me and the boys, a dozen yards of sand and polypropylene bags tarped down in back. The boys want to hightail it as soon as we drop off the sandbagging supplies, but I made up my mind well before we left Texas. So long as volunteers are out preparing for Zeta's arrival, I plan on being one of them. The boys seem to think this goodwill of mine is just some PR stunt, me angling for the next deal. I've never pulled this kind of shit before, they say, so why now? And I'm trying to tell them: I feel like I've got unfinished business here, like I owe this place something, though I'm not sure what.

To say we're swimming against the current would be an understatement. Every other car is headed off the island, practically bursting with suitcases and valuables. Beyond them, the island's stilted structures—houses, restaurants, and hotels—line up like dominoes. In five days, when the first helicopter news crews can make it out to survey Zeta's aftermath, I'll see for myself how few of them remain standing, the rest strewn as splintered wood across an island torn in two. But for now, Rose Isle's still whole, its buildings intact.

We keep arguing, my crew and I, until they begrudgingly drop me off at a volunteer tent halfway down the island. As they unload supplies—having long ago learned to swallow their gripes within earshot of clients—I hop out to introduce myself to the on-site coordinators. And that's when I see Tara.

Of course, I don't know her name just yet. Right now, she's merely the woman fiddling with a shovel outside the volunteer station, watching my crew dump sand onto the bluff above the seaward beach. And though I can only see a sliver of her face, angled away from me as she is, I can tell at first glance that she's got this effortless grace to her, like she could be running on two hours of sleep and still look this poised. I try ignoring this thought—having as little time as I do for casual courtship—but by the time I'm done convincing myself I'm not attracted to her, I realize one of the volunteer coordinators is leading me her way.

"Hope you don't mind working with the other out-of-towner," he says, "All the locals got started at dawn, so y'all seemed the logical pair."

I hope the shake of my head isn't too enthusiastic in communicating that no, I don't mind. She seems not to notice as we approach, but I offer her my right hand all the same.

"Hey there," I say. "Name's Randy Kirk. Guess we'll be sandbagging together."

The moment she turns my way, her brows flash with what I interpret as interest. But the look's gone in a second, replaced by a blank stare that considers my outstretched hand before she shakes it. In the wind, strands of jet-black hair stream diagonally across her face. She seems a couple years younger than me—perhaps just shy of thirty—and has one of the weaker handshakes I've ever encountered, the type that goes dead in your hand. No ring. And her eyes are dark, cheerless, like they've already ceded victory to the hurricane.

She gives her first name in reply, but beyond that she's silent. Says nothing as the coordinator leads us to our workstation on the bluff, and once we're there, it's he who does the talking.

"As y'all can see, we're doing whatever we can to protect the levee hidden in this bluff." He points one arm to the ground beneath his feet and sweeps the other along the beach, where volunteers are lining the bluff's southern flank with sandbags. Throughout the day, I'll learn that the island's "burrito levee" is essentially a long sandbag, fifteen feet thick, hidden in the man-made bluff and spanning most of the barrier island's eight-mile length. At times, I'll spot it peeking out where its cover has eroded away, and it'll remind me of a dead, black snake. The coordinator continues, "Add as much as y'all can to what's already there. Pack the bags in real good, so the surf can't sweep them away. General evac's in four hours—we'll come get y'all then."

Then he's off. I try catching Tara's gaze, but it's fixed on the supplies my guys dumped here. She toes an empty bag, half scowling at the thing like it wronged her in a past life.

"He said you weren't from around here either." I jerk my head at the departing man.

She tosses me the husk of a sandbag. "Drove down from New Orleans."

"Didn't expect to meet another out-of-towner today," I say,

confused by her gesture but willing to let it slide. "You got family here or something?"

"Work used to take me down here." She jabs her shovel into our sandpile and swings a spadeful of it in my direction. It takes me a second to understand what she's doing, but then I fuss with the bag to get it open. She drops the sand inside before digging in again.

I wait for her to return the question, but we're wordless for two, three shovel-and-fill cycles. "I'm from Dallas, by the way," I say. "Here on business a lot—this here's my sand, actually."

"Your sand?" she repeats, cocking an eyebrow as a breath of wind crescendos.

"What I mean is, I'm in sales. I sell sand, gravel, and related accessories." I give the bag I'm holding a shake. "Like these durable rascals." From there, I tell her the whole story: how the mayor of Rose Isle called me up two days ago, desperate for supplies when Zeta's path changed. How my crew and I managed to round up a few truck-loads of material from West Texas and cart it here just in time. How I decided to help with the readiness efforts along the way. I expect at least a lick of positivity in response, but as Tara shovels, I notice she's glancing now and again at the beach below.

"See, we don't recommend using local materials in these situations," I add. "The erosion'll be bad enough as is."

"Better to burden more than one ecosystem."

"That's what I'm saying. Speaking of, I've got quite the history with this place. A couple years back, after the last storm, this beach had pretty much eroded away, so my team helped restore it. Desert sand's no good for beaches, of course—too fine—but I brought in the arm of our business that does dredging services, and they scooped up sand from beneath the Gulf to fashion a new beach out of. Pretty neat, huh?"

"Neat indeed." She gives me a once-over. "I imagine that was fairly complex to pull together. You must be quite the smooth talker."

"I suppose," I answer, my words tentative. In any other situation, I'd think she was flirting, but there's no playfulness to her, the face before me as stony and unreadable as one of those carved ancient glyphs. "I mean, there were limited funds and a competing project someone else was trying to push through. But when you've been at this for years, building relationships on the coastal protection authority and town council, you learn how to grease wheels and dance around the typical proposal process. So, in the end, we got the contract, and the town got its beach back. Win-win."

It's here I finally get a reaction from her besides the typical deadpan, a single-syllable cackle escaping her lips. Stunned to silence, I question her with a look, and she says, "No such thing as a win-win. Someone's always losing out."

I consider contesting the point but don't feel like picking an argument so soon. "Fair enough," I say instead. "I mean, that's life, isn't it? For better or worse, I've got a long history of disappointing competitors and those Greenpeace types." We're silent a few beats, and then something clicks. "Is that you? One of those bleeding-heart conservationists? If you were competition, I'd sure as Hell remember."

"Sure, a conservationist." She stabs the shovel deep into our sand. "Isn't that what we're doing today? Conserving?"

"I knew it," I reply. "There's always one of you lurking about, trying to gum things up before my projects even get started. All for the sake of the birds and turtles. But come on, let's take the example of this island's beach restoration: what were we supposed to do? Let the shoreline disappear? Towns like this live and breathe tourism, and money buys answers. Once you've got the local economy up and running, you'll have tax revenues enough for your whole eco-friendly wish list. But we had to fix the beach first."

"So you offered them a stop-gap solution."

"Exactly. You get it. That's what I'm always telling my clients: I'm a solutions guy. Got a gap in need of stopping? I'm your man."

She says nothing further, the slightest smile creeping onto her lips, and this time I let the conversation ebb. A couple seconds later, though, she stops working, forehead creased with thought. I watch her study the waves, sandbag still cradled between my hands, and say, "What's the matter? You want to lecture me about the birds and turtles?"

"No." She resumes shoveling. "I'm just wondering how much of this beach will be gone again once Zeta's had her say."

I have no answer, reluctant to admit I hadn't yet connected those dots. At least, not consciously. But the more I churn through her words, the closer they'll ring to that feeling of indebtedness that drove me onto this bluff today. And thirty-six hours later, I'll obsess anew over that connection while watching coverage of the storm from my hotel room a couple hundred miles inland. By then, news networks will have just received word of Rose Isle's destruction. Reports will be fuzzy at that point, cobbled together from whatever details will have trickled out from beneath the oppressive blanket of a raging cyclone, so the channel I'll be tuned into will illustrate the devastation using a hastily prepared, computer-generated image.

The animation will show the island from above, as a sliver of brown—only 3,000 feet at its thickest—amid a menacing field of blue, with the burrito levee appearing as a thin red line running along its seaward side. As the reporter yammers on about a breach, a gap will appear in the line, near its middle. He'll note that once the levee's synthetic exterior is compromised, the sand inside does nothing to stop the storm. He'll compare the emptying levee to a packet of sugar poured into swirling water. And then, we'll all watch the gap grow wider and the brown give way to the blue, begging me to imagine the island's silty soil eroding into the furious Gulf, wave by wave.

I've never seen a town come together as it does on the brink of disaster. The entire island buzzes with frantic energy: trucks shuttle-running the length of it to top off supplies, volunteers carrying sandbags every which way. I'm admittedly worried by the sheer number of people who haven't yet evacuated but remind myself that hurricanes are a part of life here. Some of the older residents have probably ridden out several, through choice or necessity. They'll be okay, I tell myself. They'll all be okay.

Tara and I get into a decent rhythm, too, filling bags at a healthy clip once we've worked past our initial friction. Along the way, I manage to coax some halting conversation from her, and before I know it, she's even volunteering information unprompted: about her life in New Orleans, about the city planning job she started a year back, about how she lives with "roommates" (and, therefore, not a boyfriend). And sure, she's still hard-to-please as ever, but I don't mind. Compared to all the fake personalities I deal with in sales, her frankness strikes me as refreshing.

After an hour, we've built up a decent reserve of ready-to-deploy sandbags, and I start hauling them to the beach. It's there I come to understand what the coordinator meant by "pack them in." At the base of the bluff lies a tightly set row of 3,000-pound bags, from a contract that isn't ours, put there by the National Guard and its heavy machinery. Wedged between them and the bluff's steep, seven-foot incline are piles of sixty-pounders, like mine and Tara's, but this backup layer's a complete mess, each bag evidently flung there. People have even taken to throwing large rocks into the gap, apparently unaware that their sharp edges can tear into sandbags and render them useless.

I tell Tara about the stones on one of my trips back up the bluff. "There aren't enough to make a huge difference. I just wish it was something people knew not to do."

But she only shrugs, looking out to the ever-roughening seas. "Doubt it'll matter. Hurricane-force waves can exert what, over 4,000 pounds per square foot, pressure-wise? And these bags are—" she kicks a full one "—fifty pounds each?"

I blink at her, a silent correction the first thing that comes to mind: *Sixty, actually*. But then the meaning of her words sinks into my brain folds, and I feel this sickening warmth rising inside me, like shame and nausea had a baby. "But I'm packing them in," I stammer. "Like the coordinator said. Behind the wall of 3,000-pounders."

"Yeah, and once the waves get past that, these little things will be as good as useless." Her gaze flits to our supplies, and her face furrows just like before, back when she first looked them over.

"You knew as soon as we started working, didn't you?" I ask. "The second you saw what I brought, you thought all this was pointless."

I take her silence as confirmation.

"What about them?" I add, pointing to the townsfolk scurrying to and from the beach. "Do they know? When the mayor called, I told him what I was bringing. Said I sure as Hell couldn't get an excavator for more of those 3,000-pounders. You think he—"

"I'm sure he knows. He's probably desperate and working with the best he's got. Same with the volunteer coordinators. As for the rest of the locals, well—" she pauses to watch them work "—why bother with security theater if the audience doesn't believe?"

I turn to the town as well. At the next sandbagging station over, two middle-aged women swap jokes as they shovel. "Look," I tell Tara, "I sold all this stuff at cost. Paid for the shipping out of pocket, too. So, it's not like I'm profiting off—"

"I never said I blame you. Not for today. Not for these." She lifts an empty bag with her shovel and drops it. Midway through its descent, a gust grabs it, opens it like a sail, and sends it cartwheeling into town. We watch it go in a private vigil that ends when it disappears beneath a stilted home. And I worry our partnership's over then, that there's nothing to do but pack up, but when I turn back, Tara's nosing her shovel into our sandpile. "Well," she says, "here's to the illusion of control."

So I, too, resume my work. And though I no longer have the

same spring in my step, in time I find a whisper of hope still inside me, claiming she's nothing but a doomsayer. As today bleeds into tomorrow, that voice will stay with me. Even as I watch Zeta's news coverage, rife with those cheaply rendered graphics, I'll cling to the possibility that the early reports are overblown. But in the days following the storm, videos of it captured by survivors will surface online, and my last strands of optimism will snap. Each clip will be dark, shaky, and horrific, illustrating the carnage in a way death tolls and property damage estimates never can. From one, I'll even learn what it looks like when soil slips out from beneath a home. At the beginning of the video, the house's stilts will have already started their slide. The whole structure will remind me of an alien creature, maybe some long-lost relative of the giraffe, learning to walk as it meanders gulfward. There will be a certain grace to it, even, and for a moment you'll think everything will be all right: it'll find its sea legs and root down somewhere new. But then the stilts will hit something solid beneath the storm surge and break row by row, sending the whole structure tumbling into the waves. From there, its remains will keep skating, keep sliding, as the current pulls it to sea. And all throughout, you'll hear someone screaming over the sound of wind and water, "My God, that's the Landreaus'! They're still in there! They're still in there!"

But this will be before I've memorized the exact count of Zeta's victims: twenty-seven on that island alone. Their names and faces will not yet be seared into my brain—Ally Landreau, 7 years old with a gap-toothed grin; Ellison Chambers, 72, chess FIDE master; Karleigh King, 33, bank manager, pregnant with twins. No, this video will be posted only days after my trip to the island, and at that moment, though my grief will be guilt-tipped, I'll still be shielding myself with a warm cloak of good intentions.

After our heart-to-heart, conversation comes easier to Tara and me. It's not all smooth sailing, of course; her answers are cryptic whenever I ask about her work on the island or how a city planner knows so much about hurricane waves. I don't force the issue, though, and she, in turn, uses a lighter tone when she disagrees with me, so the push and pull to our relationship feels healthier, necessary even.

We keep working for three hours more, and then, once the

thicker bands of clouds have reached us and waves have almost swallowed the beaches, coordinators in pickup trucks swing by to relay the final evacuation order. By this point, I've become the embodiment of my profession: sand in my socks and shoes, sand coating every inch of my clothes, sand gritted between my teeth. Tara's in the same position, though, and not making a show of it, just picking the gloves off her fingers as she gazes to the horizon. So, I stand shoulder to shoulder with her and do the same.

"You know," I say, "I was thinking about everything you said, what little we could do today, and it reminds me of a joke we tell on my crew. We always say we should offer our clients unlimited time. Then, all we'd have to do is take one of those old-fashioned hourglasses and jerry-rig a contraption that automatically takes sand from the bottom and puts it back up at the top. Boom, unlimited time." I sigh. "If only we had something like that now."

"And then, let me guess," she replies, "your solution would be more sandbags?"

"Why not? Big ones, this time. Enough to cover the whole island."

This draws a chuckle. "You're a model salesman, Randy. A sandbagger through and through."

At this, she makes like she's about to go, grabbing the day pack she left a few paces away. And though I'm not sure what she meant by that comment, or where things stand between us, I choose then to forge ahead with an idea I've been considering all day: the only way I've thought of to continue unspooling this absolute riddle of a person.

"So, hey," I say.

She turns to me, a twist of confusion on her face. "You need something?"

"Look, I know we didn't get off to the best start. And I certainly don't get the impression you'd ever need a few yards of sand or related accessories. All the same, I was wondering if you might consider giving me your number. I'm by New Orleans a lot and can be quite the gentleman in more everyday circumstances."

She doesn't speak for a few seconds. She seems to be smiling, which I interpret as positive. But when I look into her eyes, they remind me of burning coals, and if there are patterns to read in their smoldering, I don't consider myself oracle enough to try.

"You already have it," she says, patting me on the shoulder as she walks past. "Nice working with you this time."

I have no response, confused as I am, but I'll do a lot of thinking about that line in the coming weeks. That night in my hotel room, I'll check every pocket of my sand-covered clothes for some stray note she might've slipped in there. The whole time, I'll be thinking about what a fantastic story it'll be when I find her number among all that sand, the kind worthy of a Hollywood romcom.

But there won't be anything there. I won't figure out what she means until weeks later, when restoration work has already started on the half-sunken island. One morning, I'll be sitting in my Dallas apartment, cleaning up my inbox before work. There'll be an email from my manager sitting there, and I'll discover—to my annoyance—that it's about Rose Isle, about Zeta. His first on the subject because, to him, my only connection to this place boils down to a few figures on a quarterly spreadsheet. And sure enough, the email will say, "really sad to see," and "makes you stop and think," but also, "might be good to reach out, when the time feels right, and see if our services might be of value."

But the article he'll link to will pique my interest, and as I read it, I'll remember my boss's habit of skimming past important facts. Because below its report on Zeta's havoc, the article will detail a "series of missteps" committed by the state Coastal Protection and Restoration Authority in the lead-up to the storm. Its author will allege that an internal memo from within the Authority, written three years ago, acknowledged that the island's levee wasn't strong enough to withstand anything harsher than a Category 2 storm. The article will describe an ambitious project the Authority considered as a result, to revamp the island's defenses by reinforcing the burrito levee and installing breakwaters offshore. It'll note that the plan gained traction early on but was ultimately shelved in favor of what the author will call "vanity projects and patchwork repairs."

As I read on, one other aspect of the column will catch my eye: a last name I'll be positive I'll have seen before. Overland. She'll be the article's main source, someone who worked closely on the levee revamp project. Someone who resigned in protest when her brain-child was scrapped. And when I scroll back up to find her full name, there it is: Tara Overland.

By this point, with my mind connecting dots it would rather leave disparate, I'll search my inbox for her and unearth an email from two and a half years ago, one confirming all the dark possibilities sprouting in my brain. In some ways, its tone will be unfamiliar, belonging to a less jaded woman than the Tara I met, but the voice will be unmistakably hers:

Hi Randy,

You don't know me, and I feel like a fool writing this, but my superiors seem to value your opinion quite highly. So, here we are.

I know you're trying to build momentum around a beach restoration project on Rose Isle, and I'm sorry to say we're on opposite sides there. There's some important, potentially life-saving work that needs doing on that island concerning its hurricane defenses, which likely won't go through if your beach deal does.

I understand you're a businessman, with your own priorities, but I imagine we can reach a win-win arrangement here. So, please give me a call. I'd appreciate the chance to work together.

Best,

Tara Overland

Project Manager, Coastal Protection and Restoration Authority

O: (504) 555-9230 C: (504) 555-3422

For the first few reads, I won't believe it's real. I mean, sure, it'll look familiar, but the implication behind her tactfully chosen words—that she would've brought me in as a supplier if I'd endorsed her project—will be so clear I'll have difficulty accepting that I could've just ignored her plea. The evidence in front of me will leave no other possibility, yet that logical conclusion will be so repulsive, so contrary to everything I've thought myself to be, that I'll reread her message seven, eight times in search of some complication or catch within it to explain away my actions. But no. I'll find no such salvation. Instead, the more I stare at the email, the more I'll realize just how easy it would've been to see it appear in my inbox, skim it over, and pay it no mind. How logical it would've been, then, to ignore her number whenever she called to follow up. How inevitable that this entire episode would slip from my memory in time.

I'll consider calling her then. To apologize. I'll think about it a good long while, in fact, dialing half her number several times. Eventually, though, I'll realize I'd be doing so for my sake, not hers. So, instead, I'll head to my apartment's second-story balcony. It'll be raining that day—another of those isolated thunderstorms we've been getting more of—and I'll stand out there for hours, missing work entirely, searching for a rainbow that'll never appear.

But right now, I'm on the bluff above the levee, stretching out my final moments on this doomed island to watch the Gulf dance. Behind me, some locals congratulate each other on a job well done, and my boys are yelling for me to get in the truck, but for all intents and purposes I'm alone. I find myself thinking about my hourglass joke, and I know it's stupid, but I wish more than ever I had something like that. Because then, I could keep sandbagging as long as I need. I could fix just enough of our mistakes to help the island's defenses hold. And maybe, if I do it all correctly, the storm would keep spinning beyond the horizon, a monstrous force forever held at bay.

Kevin J. Binder is a writer of fiction and non-fiction whose work has been published in *Reckoning*, TDotSpec's *The Science Fiction Tarot*, *McSweeney's Internet Tendency*, and elsewhere. He received his MFA in creative writing from George Mason University, where he won the Shelley A. Marshall Fiction Award and the Alan Cheuse Nonfiction Award. He currently lives in New York City with his amazing wife, Erin, and their rowdy menagerie of potted plants.

Nightmare

Kelsey Dean

I wanted to throw my arms around the thick white neck of my brother's polar bear and cry *I'm glad that you are safe from the endless water.* I wanted it to nose me, too. I wanted my palm against the fur, and the warm skin beneath. I wanted to see our bones. I wanted to know they were strong. I wanted to be unafraid of being swallowed—by the bear, or the blue night, or the holes in the weft of the world. I wanted the water to move. I wanted lapping. I wanted to hear bees in the arctic quiet. I wanted wolves. I wanted anything but that cerulean muteness, pressing and pressing. I wanted to make noise. To produce birdsong. I wanted a heart-red cardinal to fly from my throat, screaming. I wanted to keep my brother in my hands. I wanted the bear to soften and curl into the snow. I wanted slumber. I wanted my brother to sprawl on the back of his bear and point to the constellations. I wanted them to stay. I wanted to not be suddenly alone in the silent twilight that was all that was left of the world. I wanted to chase them over the crest of the pale blue hill. I wanted to be untroubled. I wanted to gather their footprints and hold them, weeping. I wanted my chest to feel unbruised.

Kelsey Dean lives in Wisconsin. Her day job revolves around airplanes but she writes and arts around as much as she can in her spare time. Her work can be found in *Gigantic Sequins*, *Southword*, *Asimov's*, and *Wizards in Space*, among other publications. She sometimes posts art on her instagram (@kelseypaints).

This is not a love poem

Alexandra Dawson

As I walk past the sex store downtown, I think
of flags, how the zealots strap them on and
screw us. I am not interested in the fire

of your want, unless you want to stop
this world from burning, unless you want
to topple the men from their mountains

of heads, their slot machine eyes spinning and
spinning and spinning. No, this is not a love
poem. I will not crawl through the trenches

of your longing. You can sob all you want,
and still, the icebergs cry harder. No one
ever told them that sadness makes you

disappear. The truth is, I simply couldn't
do it. How could I write about love at a time
like this? But I guess, I did love the idea

of us, once. A daring species. A people made
of poetry. The way I used to run after stray
kindness. My delight when I reached out

to compassion, and felt it grab me back. The time
a stranger held my hand at a department store,
enclosing my fingers in hers like they were tiny

tender petals. Or when we all lay on the ground,
six of us, like landed seals, trying to coax that
cat from out beneath the streetcar. How funny

is this life, that once the cat was rescued, we
all stood up, dusted snow from our coats and
continued on our way.

Alex Dawson is a writer, mom, wildlife photographer and ESL teacher from Toronto. She recently published a nature fact poetry anthology entitled *Upon Learning That* and published her photo-poetry book, *All these Living Things*, in the summer of 2024. Alex has also been published by *The Queen's Quarterly*, *The Bombay Literary Review*, *The Turning Leaf Journal*, Livina Press, and *Gather Poets*. She writes with constant curiosity and a desire to examine the threads of connection between nature, culture, politics and identity. Alex can be found on Instagram and Substack @alexdawcreates.

Love in the Time of Te Rāhuinui

Hiria Dunning

Ko wai ka kite i te hua o te kuaka? / Who has ever held a godwit's egg?[1]

Not I. And I never will, I expect.

This whakataukī about having faith in unseen forces has become a bitter pill for me to swallow. The godwits lay their eggs in Alaska, then summer in Aotearoa from September to March every year. And in the time of Te Rāhuinui, also known as the Global Ecological Restrictions, we flightless birds are constrained, never to see Alaska, or Morocco, or anywhere else.

I shouldn't be watching *Casablanca* tonight. It's fouling my mood, despite today being the start of my doctoral research term at the Kuaka Coastal Recovery Centre. Even in a film about struggling to escape a place amidst a terrible war, the people on the screen had more freedom to move then than we do now. We must curtail frivolous luxuries for the good of Earth's systems, I know. Yet I cannot avoid the twin pangs of want and guilt when I see the pamphlets on screen: *Free France.*

Not too long ago, I was walking through Rangipuke Park by the uni (Dad still calls it Albert Park by accident). Someone shoved pamphlets under my nose: *Free Aotearoa! End the Unjust Rāhui!* Despite part of me wanting to explore the idea of a legal challenge to open the world up, there was something about the woman holding the pamphlet. It was in her eyes, a rabidness that turned me off. I scurried away before I got drawn in. When I walked past the park later, wardens were chastising the pamphleteers for wasting resources.

"My dear Rick, when will you realise that in this world today isolationism is no longer a practical policy?" Preach, Signor Ferrari.

Teagan, fellow doctoral candidate, enters our shared bedroom, immediately scoffing. "That's right. They warned me: 'Ingrid watches the same damn films all the time.'"

"So? Watch. You never know, you might enjoy it."

She does so, hunched beside me on my bed so she can see the tiny screen of my laptop better. But after a while, something stirs her from her seat. "Sorry, 'Grid. I can't do it. I can't watch things from that

1. Traditional Māori whakataukī (proverb)

long ago. It always makes me wonder . . . didn't they see this coming? Doesn't it make you mad?"

"I'm allowed to like what I like. My Dad's an old film buff. It rubbed off."

"Fair enough." She slips over to her bunk and chooses a heavy tome from her bedside nook. For all she mocks me, her taste in books seems equally continental and twentieth century. Tonight, she's reading something called *Love in the Time of Cholera*. Pleasant.

Much like having to put up with Te Rāhuinui, I'm going to have to put up with Teagan for the next six months. That's a sacrifice I'm willing to make, to be with the creatures I've devoted my doctorate to: the Eastern bar-tailed godwit, or kuaka.

SEPTEMBER

They arrive with tired, heavy grace, in a huge formless mass like static on an old TV screen (something Dad explained to me, when it happened in an old movie, because I had no idea what the fuzzy black and white meant). With their wings spread in the air, their shape makes sense: the darkness on the wings balancing the white underbelly, the spread of wing-to-tail-to-beak an elegant, pointed geometry.

Then they land, and it is all comedy.

Wings drooping on the ground, they sweep around the shore like dowagers and old maids entering a ball, the excitement of their arrival all gone. We workers are the suited-up gentlemen awaiting these feathered dames, excitement coursing through us as they land. We can only watch, for now. Later, the real work will begin, treading gently in the dance.

It is my job, once the new arrivals have settled in for the night, to walk around following the quiet ping of my sensor. There is an old saying that the kuaka carry a stone in their mouth which helps them find their way back here every year. I don't know about that, but some of them do carry a secret. Certain birds have data pegs tucked away in their tags, replete with communications from the teams in China, Japan and Alaska. The files on the pegs can be gathered from two metres away. Once all the pings on the sensor have vanished, I've collected all there is to collect, and I head in for the night.

In the morning, I analyse the data collected. Plenty of it has been sent over the academic web already, backed up on the pegs to ensure the message comes through correctly; this hen was injured by illegal fishing nets in the Huang Hai Sea, but made a full recovery;

that male has an aggressive streak, proceed with caution; records of diseases and injuries; breeding statistics; nicknames, even, for individual birds.

Then something unexpected catches my attention. A video file labelled *Hello from Alaska.* I open it up to see a tanned and freckled face under a shock of red-brown hair. The man breaks into a smile that transforms his whole face from boyish to bright. When he speaks, his voice is loud, with an accent I've only heard in old movies.

"Hey there! I have no idea who this message is going to reach, but I don't know, I just feel kinda compelled to reach out across the world and say hi from the Yukon-Kuskokwim Delta in Alaska. My name's Noah, I'm twenty-six, and I'm a biologist—well I mean, that's obvious, probably, to my audience, whoever you are. Hopefully you speak English, because I highly doubt my message will find a Yup'ik speaker across the world.... But anyway, I wanted to reach out across the GER, say Hi, get to know someone who lives different from me, because life is awful protracted around here. Anyway, what to say...uh...."

He shifts in his seat, uncomfortable, and I'm nodding along as if to give him a positive social cue, *keep going.*

"To be more specific, I'm a Research Team Lead here in the Yukon Delta Reserve. Because of the protected status of the teguteguaq—the godwit, that is, in my indigenous language, Yup'ik—because of that I'm one of a very small bunch of people allowed to live in this place on the Delta. I winter nearby too, living on reclaimed tribal land."

He shares some photos of the birds in situ. The images are a window into another world, where the grey birds are transformed. When breeding season hits, they turn reddy-brown. It's funny to think how the same birds we both care about are so different in the two places.

"So, I love birds, obviously. Godwits are just...like, do you get what I mean when I say I love how stupid they look sometimes? That way they drag their wings after landing.... It's enough to make my eyes water, trying to keep myself from giggling in front of my colleagues. It's like they've got big sweeping skirts on, don't you think?"

He's looking off past the camera, his eyes bright, his smile wide again. I'm nodding along and laughing. *I do think they look like big sweeping skirts!*

"Anyway, what else to say...I play guitar—not well, but I enjoy it. I love old music. I mean like, stuff that's coming up on its second centenary. Don't judge me. But ooh, let's see, can I recommend anything, in case you're interested. Well, all right, let's start really 101 beginners here, some classic Rat Pack, and say... Frank Sinatra. If you can get your hands on some of his music, I think you'll be pleasantly surprised.

"So, uh, yeah... if you find this, whoever you are, why don't you consider saying Hi from your side of the world? I'd love to get to meet someone I'd never meet otherwise. So, piuraa! Which means goodbye, or 'stay as you are'."

MARCH

"Hi Noah, kia ora. It's nice to meet you. My name's Ingrid Rawiri, and I'm twenty-four. I come from Tāmaki Makaurau, Aotearoa, but while I'm doing my doctorate, I summer with the godwits down the coast."

I've watched Noah's message again and again, all three minutes and fifty-six seconds of it, who knows how many times since that day, over the weeks and months intervening.

I agonised over months about what to say to him. Would it be too weird if I went all out? Too late. I'm going all out.

"So, this is labelled video #1, even though I'm recording this just before the godwits take off. After I saw your message in September, I started collecting stuff to show you. It's all numbered chronologically, but you can ignore that if you want and just browse."

There was no rush to respond in September, no way to rush anyway. He'd sent it over the data pegs, without backing it up on the web. He hadn't attached an email address or any other way to get in contact. Nor should he have, given the academic nature of such an address. We are supposed to conserve international web resources for essential things. Random pen pal relationships are not included in that. So that meant I'd have to rely on Air Godwit to deliver my response to this contraband message of Noah's.

With all that time between, I collected images and short videos of the godwits, of our work, the land, even our parties. I curated an interesting package to send across the world. I even had all my colleagues wish him a Happy New Year on video.

"I managed to find some Frank Sinatra." Dad had complained about the hassle of hunting in old music archives and mailing the data peg to me through the university's internal system. "Actually, it became a whole rabbit hole for me, chasing down the whakapapa—the ancestral lines—of the different songs of his, because it seems like those guys back then were always covering each other's music. I ended up falling in love with Bing Crosby's version of *I'll be Home for Christmas*. You should check that out.

"Anyway, would love some more music recommendations if you've got any. As for me, I'm an old film buff, so I'd like to recommend some classic cinema if you've got the time for it. Bear in mind, please, some of these are very 'of their time'. But I would have to recommend *Casablanca*, definitely—I was named after Ingrid Bergman—and I suppose *Singing in the Rain, Wizard of Oz* and *Seventh Seal* are big favourites of mine too."

I worked the intervening months between September and March, caring for any ailments of the godwits, tracking their numbers, health, growth, and various other important stats we want kept. And I took *lots* of photos.

"We call the GER Te Rāhuinui here. I wonder how tough you find living under it? I wish I could travel the world, like our feathered friends. Still, in the absence of that option, I guess I'm going to make sure they can keep on keeping on!

"Oh, and by the way, we have something like 'piuraa' for goodbye down here too. It's 'E noho rā' which means goodbye, but also like . . . 'you keep sitting there'." I'm laughing at myself. I have to turn this damn camera off.

The godwits are already exhibiting pre-flight behaviours. For a few days now they've been fluffing up their feathers, calling to each other in that certain way that means, "Oi, let's get on with it." I leg it down the dunes, my sensor tuned to find the bird that carried Noah's message before.

There she is, with a mate, stocking up on rich pipi under the sand. Not that I can see past where her beak is dug in, searching. I stand as close as I dare, hoping not to spook her, sending my video sailing invisibly onto her data peg.

They take flight the next morning. I stand amongst my own human flock, blending in, my secret message hidden so well I can't even tell which one of those hundreds of birds bears it. After the party that night, and the clean-up the next morning, we board our transit and hover back to the university. I'll spend the next six months doing the other half of my duties for my doctorate in kaitiakitanga, including education and promotion of the kuaka and protective measures.

SEPTEMBER

Half a year later, I watch the arrival again with more experienced eyes. The numbers in the flock are growing. Our work here and across the globe is making its mark.

I'm so caught up in the energy of the arrival that it's not until the next day I notice the package on the data peg of a bird nicknamed "Ginny". *Hello again from Alaska.* It's big, a compressed file filled with a whole series of videos. I open #1.

A year on, not much has changed about Noah. His hair is longer, his freckles a bit darker this time. "Hi, uh . . . Ingrid. I gotta tell you, I almost forgot I even sent that message a year ago, so to get a response . . . and damn, the effort you went to, all those photos and videos? I'm totally grateful. Really nice to meet you."

There is something different about him knowing my name this time. This isn't just some random greeting across the world. This is him, talking to me.

"So, I watched the films you recommended. *Singing in the Rain* was pretty good, and *Wizard of Oz*, like . . . wow! But my favourite is definitely *Casablanca*. It's shot up pretty high in my personal movie rankings. Thanks for introducing me to it."

I'm smiling, and I'm clutching my elbows, and my heart is doing a flip in my chest. This is silly. I'm silly.

"And uh . . . maybe you get the joke, about what I named our bird. Ginny. Do you get it?" He pauses for effect, and I blink back, blank. "*Out of all the gin joints in all the towns in all the world . . . .* " His laughter is music to my ears. "Get it? Ginny, gin joint . . . . " He sighs, his embarrassment at himself leaking through the screen.

No, go on Noah. I get it. I get you.

"I sure wish we could meet in real life." He sighs, and my heart sighs along with him.

This video is a long one. I listen to his descriptions of what the GER is like up in Alaska. It turns out there are extra layers of difficulty in North America. The attempts to find a path to co-governance were harder there. Even between well-meaning parties, everything got to be a bit of a bureaucratic tangle, and that's before the Republic of Calvary rose up and threatened everyone else with their extreme demands for a return to "liberty". I would laugh, if not for how serious Noah is about it. To me, this all sounds like the politics of decades ago, but to him it's still so real, so close to home.

He's kept a whole string of video logs and photos. I'm treated to greetings from most of his colleagues; long panoramas of the huge delta mudflats stretching far to either horizon with cinnamon-plumed godwits busy raising the next generation; and little slices of Noah's life. He fills me in on his year since his first message and regales me with tales of his favourite godwits. I note the names down to track them later.

In one of the videos he starts a rivalry with me, calling the Yukon-Kuskokwim Delta the godwits' "real home". "Excuse me," I say in a cheeky video back to him, "but the godwits summer in Aotearoa for a longer period of time than they spend in Alaska, I will have you know." But I already know what he'll say back next year: they make their babies in Alaska, so that makes it really home, their birthplace. Fair enough.

I hunt down his music recommendations. In return I recommend another run of old cinema, bringing the focus back to Aotearoa by suggesting the works of Taika Waititi and others.

The video file which gets the most replay is his final video. Instead of a simple goodbye, he grabs an acoustic guitar from off-screen. He starts to sing in this clear tenor, so different from the deeper drawl of his speaking voice. *"You must remember this . . . a kiss is still a kiss . . . a smile is just a smile . . . The fundamental things apply, as time goes by . . . . "*

I can't help it. By the time he finishes the song and bids me goodbye—*"Here's looking at you, kid"*—I'm smiling, laughing, and there are tears in my eyes.

MARCH

I may have annoyed Teagan by playing all this old-fashioned music recommended by Noah. For Kirihimete, she gave me headphones.

"So . . . what are you sending back to gorgeous Noah, hmm?" I ignore Teagan, but this is a mistake. "He could be a deep fake, you know. You might not be talking to some cute Alaskan. He could be some filthy old guy."

"Teagan . . . . "

"Shouldn't send nudes, in case Ginny gets intercepted—"

"Auē, Teagan. Will you shut up!"

Teagan cracks up, and rolls over, eyes still trained on her book. "Oh, I'm sorry, after being subjected to hearing his music all season, I'm not allowed to comment? Putting up with you mooning over this unattainable guy for the last six months—"

"I'm not mooning—"

Oh no. I really have been, haven't I?

She can see from my face that she's touched a sensitive spot. "'S'all good, 'Grid. Forget I said anything."

I wait until she's gone to record my message to Noah, too raw to speak in front of her. I've got a bit of a script, some bullet points I want to hit in response to his last message. I don't trust my memory, especially not after what Teagan has made me face. I tell him all about my year, give him a little rundown of the other files on the peg. I don't have a talent to share with him, nothing to make his heart soar like mine did at that song.

"If only we lived in another time, huh? Maybe we could have met in person." My cheeks are burning, and I'm laughing at myself. I hope this comes across as normal, not creepy. "Pity about being half a world away from each other. But I just wanted to say, I really look forward to your messages, so . . . please keep sending them. Ka kite anō."

SEPTEMBER

Six months of burning with embarrassment and frustration and ennui, and here I am again, stalking the dunes for *Ginny—1 new packet.*

The computer room is blessedly empty. No one to hear me come crashing in, shoving the sensor's connectors into the first computer by the door, breath hot and heavy from running in the brisk night air by torch- and moonlight. I've forgotten to turn the lights on. With just my torch and the screen to show me the way, I click down the path that leads to the face I want to see.

For Ingrid is the title this time. As if to tell all others with access to the data peg to stay out of this.

His face is not smiling as brightly this time, his eyes furtive. "Ingrid . . . hi. Well, I hope this is Ingrid, anyway, because I'll be mighty embarrassed if this makes it into someone else's hands . . . .

"Listen, Ingrid . . . would you consider . . . maybe trying . . . to come up to Alaska? I don't know how you'd manage it, obviously. I looked into options for me to come down to Aotearoa—" I wince at the way he wraps his American mouth around the unfamiliar syllables "—but movement here is really restricted. I wasn't able to find out much about the travel options from your country, but . . . well, what I'm trying to say is that, in the world before this one, I would have tried to meet you, to see if this thing I feel going on between us is something that could . . . you know . . . Because really, in-person chemistry is where it's at, but I feel a connection to you already . . . . Anyway. Sorry, maybe this is all just a one-sided thing for me, in which case, just forget I asked."

No, Noah. I want to see you too.

He continues in a lighter, smilier vein, telling me all about his year. He's trying to ignore the heavy weight he just dropped. It's not until the end that he even dares to hint at anything else, when he signs off: "Well . . . *here's looking at you, kid.*"

What he asks is impossible.

MARCH

No matter how many photos I take, videos I share, moments in my life I give to him, I feel as if it all hinges around that one little sentence. I try to brush it off, contain it in just a few seconds amongst many other minutes of happy times, so it doesn't linger or taint the rest of this package I've put so much care into.

"Hey, I'm sorry Noah, but I can't leave Aotearoa."

That's it.

Te Rāhuinui rankles. And time . . . *time goes by.*

SEPTEMBER

I stare at the sensor with dead eyes.

Ginny—no new packets.

MARCH

The reason why he didn't send anything is not the one I first thought. It's worse.

There's a war on. The Republic of Calvary sent their army and navy up to Alaska in their latest bid for North American reunification. Of course Noah can't send me a message back. Maybe he never even got my message, though in the news that I can scrape off the academic web, the war didn't start until February.

I research, I fill in applications, and after that flurry of activity, I have to sit down and ask myself—because I share these thoughts with no one—do I even want to go to Alaska?

My maunga, my awa, my whānau is here. Kuaka Coastal Recovery is here, my university is here. Everything that I have learned about kaitiakitanga is specific to here. And I would be a fool to leave. Aotearoa has it so much better than so many other places in the world, thanks to our geographical isolation. Not to mention there's a war!

I mull over these doubts as I tend to our birds, maintain their environs, monitor pest defences, and wait for word to come from the Ministry of Transport.

I watch *Casablanca. "With the whole world crumbling, we picked this time to fall in love."* Yes, thanks for the reminder, Humphrey Bogart. My favourite film has me in tears now. Great.

I wish I was with Noah. I'm glad I'm not. To assuage my guilt and worry, I send as much of my paycheck as I can to Alaska to support their defence. I even rally others at the Centre, and in the surrounding towns, to do the same.

I get told off. Either because I was annoying people, or because I was wasting work time and resources. The centre manager warns me that I might not be invited back next year unless I clean my act up.

Instead of getting bitter about it, I pull my weight. I get all my work done on time, I contribute to the social life and the cleaning around the Centre. I make my apologies to anyone I have offended. Whenever my feelings get the better of me, there is Teagan to talk it through with me. By the end of season, I'm astounded to be rewarded for my efforts with a permanent position. No having to beg next year. I'll be back to see if Noah messages, if he's still alive.

I hold off on filming, waiting for my letter to arrive from the Ministry. When it arrives, the birds are already well fattened up and ready to take to the air.

"Kia Ora Ingrid,

Thank you for waiting for the results of your application to travel to Yukon Delta National Wildlife Refuge, Alaska. Our office is busy, and we apologise for any distress the long wait may have caused.

Your request has been marked as Personal, Non-Urgent. The Ministry would also like to make you aware that the region of the world you wish to travel to is currently considered dangerous for civilians due to military actions. This does not mean you have been refused, but due to the nature of your request, you will be subject to a wait time convenient to the Ministry. This could be up to twelve months under current wait list conditions."

All right, so they haven't refused me. *Free Aotearoa* are wrong: the government does let people move, but it is heavily regulated travel. Our rights have not been completely shut down. The scientist in me was trying to say this all along: the government isn't fascist; they are just asking us to make sacrifices to save the vulnerable species and environs around us.

This is fine, right? So why is there a pit growing in my gut?

"For your information, here is the estimated cost to the environment of your Personal, Non-Urgent trip:

- Enough fuel to heat an urban school for six months
- Significant risk to seals around Aotearoa and the Northern Pacific Rim (estimated death count: three adult seals)
- Risk to migratory birds (estimated death count: at least one bird, e.g. one toroa or one kuaka)

If you decide to confirm your trip and join the waiting list, please—"

I can't see through my tears anymore.

The Ministry's letter is on the desk before me as I try to hold it together in front of the camera and not cry about this man who might not even be alive to see this message.

"I've been trying really hard not to regret not coming when you invited me. Especially with the war. Sometimes I wonder, should I just go? Find out if you're alive or dead? Can I live without knowing that?"

I can barely see the blip of Ginny on the sensor when I'm searching for her to tag the video to her data peg.

I can't go. Not at that cost. Not even one godwit.

Not even with the famous line from *Casablanca* ringing in my head: "*. . . you'll regret it. Maybe not today, maybe not tomorrow, but soon, and for the rest of your life.*"

SEPTEMBER

Te Rāhuinui continues.

It will continue for the rest of my life. I will never get to enjoy the freedoms I am working so hard to realise.

The godwits arrive, cresting over the grey bulk of the dykes protecting the Hauraki plains from the encroaching sea. Ginny bears no news for me at all.

I make a decision. I won't be such a wreck this year. To quote my favourite movie, "*It doesn't take much to see that the problems of three little people don't amount to a hill of beans in this crazy world.*" I will stay strong and make a happy home for these birds who fly halfway across the world twice a year.

The godwits, and every other creature on this planet, had to put up with a couple of centuries of us utterly ruining their world. Now it's our chance to experience some fairly reasonable deprivations. I will let that be the love we send each other, from across the world. I'll show my aroha for Noah in making sure these little guys get through the Antipodean summer. I hope if he's alive, he'll do the same up in the Arctic. For now, I guess that's going to have to be enough.

DECEMBER

> *He kuaka māranganga, kotahi manu e tau ki te tāhuna, tau atu, tau atu, tau atu. / The flock of godwits have swooped up into the air, one lands on the sandbank and the others follow.*[2]

They say that the godwits could have been integral in leading the people who became Māori to find Aotearoa. The continuity of the flock has become my guiding star. Part of my whakapapa, my purpose in life. Doing everything I can for them takes the edge off.

I'm listening to my Kirihimete playlist when Sinatra's smooth tones jump out at me. "*. . . I'll be home for Christmas / if only in my dreams . . . .*"

This is prime tear-jerker territory. Maybe I need to take this one off the list.

Teagan comes crashing into my room—my single occupancy room, now that we're no longer students—and drags me out to the canteen. Everyone there stares at me as I enter. What have I done now?

She has the screen paused, ready for me to see the news item. She hits play, watches my face.

The images of a snowy war-torn place blink by without my comprehension, then footage from a refugee boat. There is a man in a huge puffer coat, handing out food to his fellow passengers. A shock of red-brown hair. Smiling despite it all.

I have not held a godwit's egg.

But I know. That's enough. For most of human history, that's all any of us get. For the kuaka, summer here, summer and eggs there: that's all they ask.

Where the godwit lands, let the others follow

"Love in the Time of Te Rāhuinui" originally appeared in Headland Journal *in December, 2023..*

2. Whakataukī attributed to Tūmatahina of Te Aupouri

Hiria Dunning (Ngāti Porou, Ngāti Kahungunu, Ngāti Raukawa, pronouns: she/her/they/them) was a mentee in the Te Papa Tupu 2024 programme for Māori writers, and hosts the weekend writing prompt #pretendpanel on Bluesky. No matter which genre playground they're playing in, whether on stage, poem, prose or gaming console, their fantastical and inclusive stories come from the heart. When not writing, Hiria enjoys collecting divination paraphernalia, laughing with/at their children, and dodging their cat's assassination attempts. www.hiriadunning.com

Camouflage

Rain Jordan

> Tell the truth, but tell it slant.
> The truth must dazzle gradually.
> **—Emily Dickinson**

I often work in slant mode. Whether through abstraction, symbolic imagery, or magical realism, I like my work to be open to more than one interpretation. This way, both the subject of the work and the work's viewer are recognized as the individual beings they are, in flux and replete with potential. I think of art as invitation to the viewer to come to their own meaning while considering the possibilities of the subject's worldview as well. For me, a slant approach to art opens access to more dialogical forms of communication.

Rain Jordan's works have been shown in the USA and Australia and are in private collections throughout the world, including New York, California, Oregon, and Australia. Several have also been featured in Saatchi-curated collections at Saatchi Art, as well as on several book covers and in magazines. Most recently, her jellyfish sculptures were featured in a juried exhibition at Cannon Beach Arts Gallery, and in early 2026 a group of her mid-century modern themed dog drawings will also be shown there.

Rain holds a BA and an MFA from the California State University, San Jose. Born and raised in California, she moved from Rio Del Mar (Santa Cruz) to the north Oregon coast in 2015 to open a dog welfare and protection nonprofit.

The Mouthful

Hank LaRose

What is up with the sky? What is up with it and the clouds and the grasses and how everyone talks? Do you know this? Why they don't stop as it goes closer to the end of the table, Jess? They could just say, "Oh my geez do you see that glass thing is nearly to fall off the table, drop and shatter on the floor?" That would at least be a step, don't you think? As the glass seesaws, deciding whether it should tip, bumping closer and closer to being like milk and glass cereal on the ground. Do you see this, Jess? That people make shape of the world and, with their gift of tongue, speak. If they wanted. Not just some ancient reptilian noise. Speak, so they may see you.

Look—I will tell you what it is if you do not know. If you will listen again. Not just pull me into the room so you may do your business. No more to line me up on the stand, slide my head through the wood, and squeeze me for what I have to give you by my body. Here I am and I will tell you. I will tell you about the clouds and the grasses and everything moving as though it were this great big before. Coming and building. I will tell you of the new grass that gives me the diarrhea. Of the voice that says rain for forty days, coming from the air like a craving. Of how people talk like nothing, like how are you guy, good sweetie, oh it's so nice to see you, yes let us convene again, maybe over lunch because we are friends. Do you feel this like me? That it is nearing? Or am I just a goat.

These are just a few that concern me, Jess, in a list of long. Truthfully it goes and goes forever, this list, so full of parts that to tell you all of this big arrival would be to blab nearly everything, and that I cannot do as time is creeping up. What I want to say quickly is that I am sorry to make myself out of dust and leave no goodbye, but I don't believe in it anymore, and I'm not sure what you would do if you saw I was leaving. You might tie me down or search the fence for the hole I've been gnawing. You would probably use it as more reason to sigh when I attempt to say something honest. Oh, Cass is too smart for her own good. Oh, she is such a bother. Oh, if she only further developed the cortex then she would know that Jess and milk is scripture. That the tongue is truth and the fence is law. But Jess, there are things I used to do that now feel as if I'm wearing tiny socks. Not that there's the low on circulation, but that I realized nearly all you have for me is socks and I cannot do so because I have hooves, Jess.

You see, with the pepperweed I tried to show you, like how we talk nearly all the time. You nod, and I say good, thank you. I lift my head through the hole, you look me in the eye, I look back at you, you smile, grab my teats, and there is love. I felt it in your hands, Jess, when you squeezed me. How you called out so we may embrace in our square room. I remember how it was young.

Last time, though, I brought the pepperweed that grows over by the creek. I tried it like usual because I enjoy the flavor more than grain, I think, since it does not show itself right away. Grain is small and pebble-like so you'd expect the crunch. Pepperweed, on the other leg, is a mustard. It is green and stemmy like the other greens that live near like the grama and buffalo grass, and if that was all you could believe or know, that all these green stemmy plants were alike, then you'd think they'd both be mild. But beneath is a quick spice and wow I am glad it grows by the creek. But this is not why I talk about it.

I brought it by the pen to show you it has a new taste, a foul taste that comes at the back of the throat. Did you know this? Also Jess, around it grew this darkened patch of plant like from some kind of fungus. As I smelled it I bumped the leaves, and they crumbled as dust. A grey stem that just dissolves into nothing. Maybe the grama or something else, I couldn't tell, up from the base and empty as it went higher, looking stable until you touched, causing the thing to poof into the wind. I swear a twist came at my throat when I saw this happen, a twist like how a cable is wrapped in loops, around and around until it's dizzy, my head. Remember not just this once, but more as I turned to look over toward the west side of the field. Over the fence on the far length of the river the peppergrass looked like nothing at all, just not there or hidden by the grama. Green hills or greenish hills with this slight bit of grey. It was around us all. This thing. Wrapping, tighter.

So I bit off a piece of pepperweed and carried it up to the barn as the early morning rain trickled and made all these puddles in the field. You were there unloading from the vehicle saying hey like it was every day with us—let's get things going. Though I was up on the fence making noise with my teeth and you said, "Easy now, Cassandra."

You never like me on the fence.

Oh I remembered your truck wailed and you brought it to the shop right away, so I tried to make that noise to be like the truck to get your eyes. Kind of high squeaky and the wheezing of the pipe. You did this within the day, I remember, straight to the shop. So I squeaked, and then of course the whole herd copied, turning my call into noise as you continued to bring the boxes indoors, now not hearing me anymore. I stopped and waited a little. I watched the puddles in the rain. I knew I would see you in the parlor at least where I could speak to you alone. The herd continued their rumble.

Not soon after that I trotted inside the barn to meet you by the gate and Peanut followed with me knowing what was coming next, the milking, yet she still made the noise like the truck. Her eyes were wide and happy because she liked the noise as it came out between her lips. This is an everyday with Peanut, the waiting by the gate in the barn, as she wants us to bang our heads together. We hit and shared our thought until you came into the milk parlor, this time wet and frustrated, as you forgot your jacket. I saw it in your movement. I clacked Peanut's head and told her about the pepperweed. She paused and then hit me back. I said yes, feeling dizzy. We stood there for a long moment, as I saw her big eyes deciding, then taking and holding the brain pieces near her chest. "Oh," she said in her face, and moved aside to let me through the gate when you first opened it. That I was grateful for, Peanut.

When we were in the parlor, Jess, I held the pepperweed in my mouth as you helped me up the stand. This while the routine brush and wipes. The room felt damp as some of the rain splashed through the window. I thought to tell you of the pepperweed in my mouth to signal. Yes, so I waved the grass around and you picked it from my mouth and dropped it on the floor. I saw it on the ground in front of me. You just threw it on the floor. Snatched it and threw it on the floor. Took it from me to put on the ground.

Then I tried something else by moving my mouth as I often see you move yours, Jess, with your lips and tongue flap. I had to bend and twist the muscles. It was like when a hinge goes the wrong way, like a leg far out of its socket. And for a second in that stretching I thought I my jaw came undone. Though I said it. I finally got the thing out. I said, "Pleeease, Jess," which caused the room to fill with it and its loudness. I felt you slow your hands. You stopped, then you looked at me like always and said in one tone, "Not right now," and continued milking.

This, I believe, hurt.

Jess, you know that I was staring to the wall, the white wall, as I felt you finish. Just the last squeezes and my head as a nothing with the white zooming in above, around me, filling. I saw that Peanut had sneezed on the wall the day before. Inside me this wanting to vomit. You had forgot to clean, so the dots were dried in a cluster and glistening and I felt the crawling up inside me like a puppet hand through to my mouth, pulling at the bones. My jaw hung swollen even though it popped back into place.

The spots on the wall seemed, for a long while, like they were moving, maybe, since they were at the end of my nose and my eyes had crossed. I could not tell. Globs would shift secretly until I was really looking and then they'd snap back. With the white still circling around. A nothing.

Then I saw you were done.

You were to let me out into the pasture as you always do, standing by the gate with it open beneath your arm, the milk room door open, my head unlatched from the block, and I waited, tall on the milk stand, as we stared for the long until you gestured to the gate. You widened like go out, Cass, go out across out in the pasture with the rain coming down. Just go out, Cassandra. I saw it bundled in your face. Another ahead, another tomorrow, the same day forever, and it was empty like a linked fence for you, tied together in a long unend. You rubbed your eyes to reach behind them the brush that won't let us be. Yet you won't stop this, day and day, because at least you can yawn and drink your drinks, at least you can pretend that you are Jess and then go home. This is what you've always said with that face, the one you hold at the end as you're waiting for me to get on with it.

So as you did this yawn and such, I ran back to pick up the grass you dropped on the floor. Maybe I would say again with Jess, look, I get it. You're tired. But I heard you come up behind me quick like I'd done something wrong. It frightened me how quick you were behind me. You snagged me and tugged me so hard by the collar that I strangled, then you pulled me around. You said, "Come on now, Cass, get out," as you always do, like just a moment before there wasn't any of that word I spoke but nothing and more sound. Then you pushed me through the hall toward the gate.

Jess, that's all for this way. Tomorrow you might call out for me in the morning when it is just dark enough to think I'm still asleep. You'll see if maybe I was in the corner behind some bale, yet as you look I won't be there to respond. It'll be quiet as you search. You might feel restless, and after a few hours you might find the hole in the eastern fence. You might say to yourself that this is some big deal while you worry for my health, feeling what you say is a kindness. That'll be true for you as truth has always been—a thing to hold like my collar. You might wonder after many days, though time will take me away for I don't know how long, or where. When I come back I will have the speaking down. Yes, and you will stop what you're doing and listen. This is the promise like the rain tonight, on all the nights when the clouds are poised. Because I will have seen the world, as far as I can wander, and will tell you in clear words that beyond your eyes, your tongue, and your hands there is something big going on, Jess, and I will bring it to you in the clearest of words, understandingly.

Hank LaRose is an English and History teacher on the Colorado Front Range. His prose and poetry have been published in *Bending Genres* and *Bare Back Magazine*. In his spare time, he loves playing soccer and staring out windows.

Dr. _____ and His Thousand Children

J. R. Staples-Ager

The Society for the Preservation of Kynish Technology is proud to present the most complete artifact ever recovered from the Genetic Archive at Yor Yan. The following manuscript owes its remarkable preservation to its inscription on flesh paper, and its entombment in a bone box set into the foundation of the building. Both paper and box resisted even the hemorrhagic bombing which rendered the Archive inaccessible to all but the hardiest Shells.

As the manuscript was rolled up, exposing the latter sections to necrosis, each section was recreated with decreasing confidence. Despite the author's unverifiable claims, our hope is that this recreation will shed light on the origin of Shell technology, as well as inform current policy on the use of Kynish relics.

<Specimen #YY1-340676>

Dr. _____ and His Thousand Children

0. Numbers (99% confidence)

Never put a number in the title. That was one of the first things I read when I set out to become a writer. Numbers confuse a story. A reader might recall a manuscript's content perfectly, but, upon describing it to a friend, struggle to recall the title. *The doctor and his . . . . The million children of . . . . Oh, it had a number in it.*

My life, unfortunately, has been all about numbers. I have had, at various times, anywhere from fifty to a thousand siblings. (I am rounding, of course. Considering Dr. _____ fertilized over 15,000 embryos—resulting in 2,972 live births, 862 numbered adults, and 59 siege survivors—you must lend me a little grace.) My father's first 347 children did not live long past maturity, and were therefore fed to the nutrient reclaimer, the same policy he used for stillborn kvennik calves. I was number 523, late enough in the progression to have relatively few defects, but not so late as to carry the burdens thrust upon his later works.

This number, 523, meant I was old enough to witness the rise and fall of the Observatory at K_____ from beginning to end. However, this story does not begin with my birth, a half-formed thing pulled from the vivisected belly of a kvennik. Nor does it end with the fall of the Observatory, that weeks-long siege with its grisly end.

It does not even end with me now, a married adult expecting

their first child. In fact, I wish not to exist in this story at all. I have been too perceived already—both by the staff at the Observatory and the soldiers, reporters, and psychologists who descended after its fall. I do not want my father in this story, either. He has loomed too large in the coverage of our family: *What drove a genius to such unnatural acts?* As if he needed to be humanized just as much as his children did. This story is not even about my siblings. Number 348 writes far more beautifully about our cohort than I, and even journalists have done a better job at listing our multitudes than I ever could.

You might conclude, therefore, that this story is about nothing. Self, father, siblings—what else could there be, apart from that grotesque family unit, curled in on itself like an ingrown nail? I have deliberately bored you, dwelling on the function of numbers in the titles of manuscripts. I have started with the least important information and worked up to the most important—then refused to reveal what that important information is. I have told you everything this story isn't, and nothing that it is.

Well then. This story is about the 1,897 burials I performed between the ages of 5 and 13. It is about E____, whom I met while attending to one such burial. It is about the anatomy of the noble kvennik, the Observatory's stunning pens, and a secret I remain unable to reveal until my death.

I suppose, in a sense, it is still about nothing.

1. Burials (92% confidence)

Psychologists asked me what it was like to bury so many of my siblings. Despite my poor socialization, I knew the truth would impact my future survival. I simply told them that it gave me nightmares, and they left me alone. There were too many of us, pulled from the carrion stink of that building, to tease out the trauma of those who were not at obvious risk.

This was not a lie, per se. Gravedigging *did* give me nightmares. But I also enjoyed it, in a very specific sense. It was a job that needed doing, and I did it. As I was one of the few among my siblings who could read, write, and speak Kynish, I might have secured a coveted indoor position. But I feared the harsh punishments attendant to the record-keeping and laboratory jobs and wished to pursue an occupation with minimal supervision.

The circumstances lined themselves up perfectly. My predecessor—Number 497, my first burial—had recently succumbed to illness, leaving the position vacant. Dr. ____ had been selecting for strength and height at the time of my conception, so my physical profile made me an excellent fit for the job. I took over from 497 in the spring after my 5th birthday. Within the first year, I had turned the blisters on my palms into calluses and the constraints of the classroom into a distant memory.

I did not enjoy it at first—in either the specific or the general sense. I would receive the bodies from 433, autopsy assistant and pusher of the corpse-carts. Plague risks were buried; those who had died naturally or been culled were processed into kvennik feed, as well as experimental nutrient slurries. I have lied by omission, painting myself as gravedigger only—I have been a butcher of meat both human and animal. In the beginning, I performed one or two burials every week, and spent most of my time feeding corpses into a pipeline modified from kvennik processing. Because the processes were so similar, I also assisted in kvennik butchery during meat season. Three years in, the number of contaminated human bodies increased, and I began gravedigging in earnest.

Those relentless years of burial were what made me start thinking about the numbers. Perhaps gravedigging might seem peaceful, if only in comparison to the lurid nature of butchery: broken pelvises, blood pooling into gutters, skin scalded with boiling water to loosen it from flesh. But it was only then, in my gravedigging days, that I was forced to confront exactly how much life was being wasted.

I could not intellectualize mass burial into components, or turn it into a completed circle with immediate results. The earth bloated; bodies swelled with rot, and the earth could not pack flat again. It called into question the fundamental premise of the Observatory: that we were a circular, private religion of progress, in which one was reincarnated in one's siblings, and everyone strived for better things.

I dug graves with a round-point shovel and digging bar and, later, an excavator purchased with great haste from a neighboring farm. There were no coffins—think of the expense of 1,897 coffins!—and the Observatory provided fewer and fewer shrouds as Dr. ____'s experiments reached their peak. This made body-handling an awkward business, all leaky mouths and flopping limbs. On a good day, a 3 by 6 span hole filled with quicklime was enough. On the worst days—I was around 12 by that time—I would dig a grave for a hundred or more bodies, douse it in kerosene, and set it on fire. It took 8 or 9 hours to dig a hole that wide and deep, even with the excavator and a dozen siblings as assistants. And the *smell*....

I have put off writing about it for years, thinking I could describe it in perfect detail, so the reader would be forced to experience it precisely as I did. But I have learned, observing the response to 348's work, that readers will imagine what they like. One journalist even asked me, *Which was the worst to bury*? I still remember the red rouge on her lips, how it stuck to the white bone of her teeth.

I was subsisting on media coverage at that point, a disabled adult with poor social skills and no real education. Even my handler, the money-grubbing old sinner that he was, was insulted by the question. *You expect my client to answer that?*

I never had the opportunity to respond, but I turned the question over in my mind for days. Which *was* the worst to bury? The small bundles of the miscarriages with their gluey consistency? The newborns with inverted lips? The toddlers, jaws melted from bone worms? The culled adults, still moving after a misfired bolt to the brain? The ones I had known? The ones I had seen from a distance, and was only now seeing up close?

I could give you individual examples, and force you to knit the general from the specific: *A translucent external pouch holding the digestive organs. Six limbs on one body, half of them boneless. A second mouth protruding from the belly, teeth degraded by stomach acid*—and so on. Or I could make you unravel the specific from the general: *I have seen more shades of red than I have a name for, because the name was the thing itself, and not everything is like something else.*

Neither, I think, conveys the scope of it. It seems more and more monstrous to tell you I enjoyed it. At the least—at the very least—it allowed me to pay my respects to the dead.

My respects were not particularly complex, mind. The way to dig a hole 6 span deep, after all, is to dig a hole 6 span deep. If they had hands, I crossed their hands over their chests. If they had eyes, I closed their eyes with a gloved thumb. If they were adults, I memorized the maturity number branded on the neck. If they were not, I memorized the birth number branded on the thigh. If I had time, I planted flower seeds stolen from the greenhouse. I fertilized them with kvennik manure, and watered them with runoff from the river.

Perhaps *respects* is not such a ludicrous term, after all. Though the Observatory is gone, I remember every number and name. I have never stopped counting. This ritual has become so ingrained in me that, during a particularly difficult period several years ago, I dug myself a hole and slept at its bottom for several nights, counting all the way up from 1,075 to 2,972, 497 to 862, and 1 to 1,897. I have since filled the hole and planted viskany flowers in the turned earth. I can see them outside my window, now, waving bright red in the wind.

Back at the Observatory, the day's hole would swallow me. 6 span down made the ground level with my head, so I had to cut shallow steps to get out. Deep within the earth, I watched myself as if from a great height. I had long since learned to keep the intense arithmetic of my continued existence—the pursuit of meals and praise, the avoidance of culling and infection—as far away from the ritual of burial as possible. On my best days, I could leave the earth entirely, and float unimpeded through the air.

This detachment, whether learned or inherent, has persisted well into my adult life. The urge to remove myself remains even while writing this story—as if it is, if you will forgive the obvious metaphor, a dead thing I am burying.

But the truth is that dead things no longer hold any horror for me. Their story is over. I owe them nothing; they feel nothing, so I am not obligated to end their suffering. There is nothing left to end. Watching the living, however—watching the living suffer—has been one of the most painful experiences of my life.

2. E___ (90% confidence)

One of the most pressing questions posed by the public was how Dr. ____ remained undiscovered for so long. He continued to publish his psychological and gynecological papers while running the Observatory, including several on the theoretical cultivation of embryos outside the human womb. And while the Observatory was remote, it nevertheless sold meat and dairy to the entire principality, requiring extensive deliveries to continue its operation. The town of K___ was only a league away. How could a place so horrible persist right under the public's noses?

There have been many rationalizations: Dr. ____ was a highly respected scientist, and deep in the pockets of the local constabulary. The Observatory had a false front, so delivery vehicles only viewed the pens reserved for the meat and dairy kvennik, not those forced to birth my siblings. High walls surrounded the property—ostensibly to keep volchanik out, but in reality to keep us in. Isn't it understandable that the public might not smell the stink of the corpse fires?

An often ignored truth is that the Observatory was both an asylum and a slaughterhouse. Nothing could have concealed it more effectively than these two facts. "The public"—blameless until the disclosure of the Observatory's true nature, outraged forever after—knew it was a horrible place and did nothing. That it was an asylum whose inmates were born and buried there was beside the point. Number 348, poster child for us survivors, has put the irony most eloquently: *We were humanized only upon the revelation of just how inhuman we were.*

While everyone knew of the venerable Dr. _____—his grand ideas, his commendable work putting unfortunates to useful labor—few people wanted to meet those unfortunates and verify his claims. Apart from the butchery of human meat, our hygienic standards were little different from those of other slaughterhouses and sanatoriums. Though his assistants were sworn to utmost secrecy, as he could easily ruin their careers, this was more formality than anything. Kyne's researchers were bent on biological improvement at the time, and while the claims of government funding have never been substantiated, I would not be surprised if our intended purpose was to become an army of cheap, obedient soldiers.

As for the townsfolk, the people most likely to realize that something was deeply wrong? They devoured the Observatory's meat and milk at heavily discounted rates, rationalizing their runoff-related diseases as no worse than they'd get in Kyne's stinking cities. Most could not afford to put food on the table without Dr._____'s charity, much less move elsewhere, making the Observatory more blessing than curse. Further, as I learned from E____, local superstition surrounding several disappearances kept them far away from the Observatory itself.

I was 11 when I met E____. I was digging a grave at the time—one of my very first mass graves, a particularly bad one. The smell was too much for me, so I had taken a break by heading to the river to get water for the flowers.

This is what saved E____'s life and, though I did not know it yet, mine. If she had followed the river into the Observatory proper—no doubt asking the nearest person about the hormone treatments used on the kvennik—she would have been knocked unconscious, shot with a captive bolt pistol, and fed to the machines. Her torn and bloodied clothes—tangled with a token arm or leg—would be found weeks later, and her death attributed to volchanik. No one would have heard of poor E____ V____ again.

I knew, because I had heard of such things happening before. But I did not make the connection immediately. When the girl came walking up the river, I assumed she was one of my siblings. Every child I knew, after all, was one of my siblings. And yet . . . I knew my siblings, and she did not look like one of them. She had bright-colored clothes, not the pale smocks worn at the Observatory, and her round face was free of hormonal augmentation. More than that, she seemed to want to talk to me.

"I'm here about the frogs," she said.

I felt a sudden vertigo, as if a chasm had opened between us. *An outsider.* An outsider was here in the Observatory. "The . . . *frogs*?"

She lifted a complicated apparatus: it bubbled with strange protrusions, like a water clock subjected to one of Dr. ____'s more extreme limb-development experiments. Apparently my stunned stare made me as good an audience as any, because she immediately launched into a lengthy explanation.

The injection of growth hormones into kvennik has long been established practice in Kyne: to increase milk yields, facilitate gestation, and hasten maturity. Runoff from slaughterhouses—urine, feces, milk, blood—has documented effects on human development, from premature birth to early death. But limits have been established to keep harm at acceptable levels, and nowhere were the effects as extreme as they were in K___.

What alerted E___ to the Observatory's transgressions was not K___'s miniscule fertility rate. It was not the early bleedings, undropped voices, or cyclopic stillborns. It was not the fact that she was born with her index finger fused to her middle finger, like a badly knitted glove. It was the frogs.

E___'s favorite species—a race of tiny green amphibians the size of her thumb—were dying. After three consecutive summers studying them—squatting by the riverside, catching tadpoles in a bucket and raising them by hand—E___ concluded that this was due to an imbalance in the sexes. Growth hormones from the slaughterhouse were causing a disproportionate number of frogs to become female—E___ was all but certain of it.

E___'s mother, a glassblower, had created the apparatus to help E___ test her hypothesis. It was part collection device, part culture tube: allowing E to gather water samples and observe their effect on the frogs throughout development. The farther water samples were taken up the river, the more the sex distribution became skewed. Frogs raised in water taken from just outside the Observatory were almost exclusively female. Growth hormones at the established limits for slaughterhouse runoff did not cause such skewed distributions. E___ was forced to conclude that either the dosage was extreme, or that different, more powerful substances were being used.

It pained her, to hurt the things she loved in order to save them. But she had written to the Observatory, as well as the agricultural and disease authorities of Kyne, all to no avail. (This lends credence to the theory that the Observatory was funded by the government. But I digress.) Without recourse from authority, she set out for the Observatory for answers.

Intriguingly, E____ did not frame her futile quest in terms of the suffering of K____. The sick children, the seemingly endless miscarriages, the families with livelihoods tied to that contaminated town—All this she painted in the lightest brushstrokes. It was only later that I learned E____'s own mother almost died bringing E____ to term. Instead, E____ spoke lovingly of the frogs: a clutch of their eggs, hundreds of tadpoles-to-be, no bigger than a thimble and transparent as glass. Their plight—the ruptured waste of unfertilized eggs, the silence where mating calls should be—brought her nearly to tears.

I felt a wave of repulsion at such juvenile emotion. Though I later learned E____ was almost precisely my age, I felt significantly older—and looked it. The powerful hormones injected into our kvennik mothers meant that most of Dr. ____'s children had adult female characteristics, regardless of age or chromosomal makeup. We also went through puberty extremely early—hence my ability, at 5, to dig a 6-span hole every day. E____ seemed to be around 2 years old, by my standards, and a prime candidate for culling. She lacked the height and muscle that would help one survive the Observatory, not to mention the common sense.

What incensed me most was how pointless E____'s risk was. She had disregarded every warning from her parents, every rule laid down by the bribed constabulary. She had crawled through the sluice gate that carried runoff from the Observatory towards K____. Despite her rubber gloves and boots, she was still covered in flecks of filthy water. She had knowingly risked her own life—and the lives of her unborn children—in order to prove a hypothesis she all but knew to be true.

It took me a long time to understand this impulse. I thought it was because she was greatly indulged in K____, an endlessly curious girl, smart as a slap and bright as a new coin. Her face was unbruised, after all, and her pockets full of spending money. This was true, but not the whole story. Nor was the fact that, so desperate was she to save the frogs and K____, she could not bear to think the consequences all the way through. I now know that her greatest reason was this: she saw no difference between her, and K____, and the frogs, and me.

I saw the seed of it then, though I could not have given it a name. She was not afraid of me, monstrous as I was, stinking of the burning fat of the dead. She was not afraid of poisoning herself, or her children, on the chance that her children's children might be free. Life was for the living, but also for those yet to live. However naive her methods, she considered herself insignificant under the weight of that responsibility. It was an ethos perversely similar to that of the Observatory: that it was right, moral even, to increase the suffering of those in the present, in order to decrease the suffering of those in the future.

When E___ had finally finished her explanation, I spoke. I had barely said anything for weeks, and my throat was roughened by smoke.

I said, hadn't she heard the Observatory was full of the insane? That we would eat her up, like hungry volchanik, and leave nothing but bones? She said she herself was hungry, and had already seen enough bones.

I was hungry, too. I ate up the unschooled movements of her mouth and eyes, so different from the blankness I deliberately cultivated. Hers was a life outside the airless realm of my thousand siblings: an uncontrolled experiment, full of leisurely conjecture and forgivable mistakes.

I should have scared her away. Every moment we stood there, talking of trivial things, I cursed myself for not doing so. I was so much larger than her, so much more aware of the harm that could come to a child at the Observatory. If I had waved my arms and screamed, beat her bloody, chased her down the river and away from the burning graves....

I did not scare her away. We talked for half an hour. I promised I would tell her the truth about the Observatory if only she never returned to the premises again. I led her to the sluice gate, and returned to gravedigging. I was punished for that half hour, but there were no further deaths that day.

E___ kept her promise, and I mine. At first, I left notes on the wall, spooling out the secrets of the Observatory. I wish I could say that I was wary, withholding. I was not. I began sneaking away at night to talk to her. I told her about the waves upon waves of cullings, how they would likely increase if she spoke to anyone—especially the constabulary. I found her superb at keeping secrets. E___ had no sense of her own personal danger, but danger to others terrified her. I suppose this was unsurprising, coming from someone who cared so deeply about frogs that she would risk permanent disfigurement to save them. It was surpassingly strange: to witness the same gleam of interest as in Dr. _____'s eyes, set to an entirely different purpose.

There was a ravenousness to E____, a starving fascination that defied all categorization.

She was brilliant. Oblivious. A shameless pedant with no sense of the listener's discomfort or endurance. When we were separated during the siege—and worse, during the months afterward—I would have burned everything I owned, I would have given every memory, just to see her again.

It's an interesting thought—to meet E____ again, having forgotten everything. Sometimes I think it might not be such a large sacrifice. We could live as we did before the siege: suspended in time, the truth indeterminate as an unhatched egg floating in one of her glass culture tubes. But how could I complete this manuscript without the numbers driving me forward?

That first day, forgetting would have been no sacrifice at all. I resented the odd little girl who had pierced the floating calm of my solitary rituals and brought me back to the contaminated earth.

3. Kvennik (87% confidence)

The kvennik is a noble creature.

Consider the ingenuity of her descent: a daughter to a daughter to a daughter, the only asexually reproducing mammal in all of Kyne. Consider her ever-productive milk glands, the accommodating cavern of her womb. Is not her usefulness a kind of nobility—to give and give, and take so little in return?

The kvennik is ignoble as sin.

Consider the inconvenience of filing her horns down to prevent goring, the hassle of making her breed true. Consider the stink of her shit, the bloody mess of butchery. Is not her dependence a sin—to take and take, and give so little in return?

Perhaps no creature seems simple when you have spent as much time with it as I have. I have witnessed kvennik exit the womb, attain adulthood, and be led to the stunning pens to be slaughtered. I have attended their feedings, surgeries, immunizations, and sterilizations. I even spent my womb-time in the belly of a kvennik. Tossing in my bed at night, I used to imagine that warm, wet dark: what would it be like, to dream of the world without ever having seen it?

I have also, it is sad to say, eaten a lot of kvennik. This means I have eaten someone's mother—my aunt, or at least "aunt" in the sense of the creature who gave birth to one of my siblings. (Squared by the fact that all of the Observatory's kvennik were genetically identical, the thought is even more discomfiting. Were they all my mother?)

I am grateful, in my own way, but cannot help but resent the kvennik's dependency, even as I defend her usefulness. When I attended high school in Y___, my fellow students would low at me, pulling the tips of their noses up so they looked like mine. Their impressions were terrible, but I can't fault them for trying. How could I expect them to view me as human, after every inhuman experiment performed by the Observatory?

While there are many similarities between the kvennik and the children they bore, none of us have any genetic link to our kvennik mothers. I was born from an egg generated from a stem cell, itself generated from a skin cell taken from one of Dr. ____'s female nurses. (This story is not about the nurses, either. Others have described the indiscriminate abuse; I feel no need to repeat it.) This arduously created egg was then injected with Dr. ____'s sperm and used to impregnate a kvennik, who was hormonally induced into a rapid 2-month gestation. Later, after I had settled in Y___, a genetic testing company offered to let me know which nurse was my second genetic parent. *It's free!* they insisted. I declined. People assume you'll want something just because it's free.

The kvennik pays nothing for her life, but pays with her life anyways. While Dr. ____ discovered that kvennik could be injected to give birth to human children as well as carry them, he also discovered that this would render them infertile and necessitate their butchery. Our "mothers," therefore, were vivisected after being stunned with a bolt to the brain, combining the two processes neatly. I have imagined this too—to be sleeping, content, and then cruelly wakened when what you think of as the whole world is sliced open. It is a startling idea: could this world, too, be sliced open? Once born, one ceases to be a victim by default, and becomes capable of cruelty—harmed, certainly, but no longer harmless.

Have I bored you to sleep yet? Are you ready to wake up?

4. Stunning Pens (54% confidence)
The quality of recreation drops sharply in this section. While its first and final portions were rolled near the bottom of the bone box, leading to improved preservation, its heavily damaged middle leaves the author's actions unclear.

My father's experiments became grotesque near the end.

Even I must admit this—I, who maintain that while what was done to us was grotesque, none of us are grotesque in ourselves. It is one thing to know you should not have been born, and another to think that, as a result, you do not deserve to live. have spoken via hand-sign to my siblings performed flesh means of translation.

Around child 790, it was no longer possible to separate the experiment f[*rom the*] person. My later siblings *appeared* [*to*] possess ideal —at least by the standards of my classmates in Y____. And their initial evaluations were from the baseline established by those of us in the 500 and 600 range. This is part of what led to the increased burials—a culling of However, these bril[*liant*] new lights did not burn long. Upon autopsy, org ans degene[*rate*] A single burst of deliberately , or some flaw in [*the*] design? I pray no one repeats his to find o[*u*]t.

I am glad to have saved E____'s life, but I have wished that she had not saved mine. At the time, this was because I was an insignificant member set. That final purge was coming, regardless of the actions of a gravedigger and their . Now, it is because of the bitter con[*sequences*] of the : the bl[*ood on m*]y hands, and [*on*] hers.

My expertise at mass burial is the reason I am alive. It saved me from the cullings during the siege, and the after. But I could no longer see any purpose to that salvation. I need not explain to you the dissonance of living solely due to others' [*deaths*].

It is difficult to explain my actions after . I have always, [*al*] ways wanted to live. If you had lined us all [*up before a*] firing squad I would have fought you, tooth, nail, and shovel. But to witness life after l[*ife*] birthed with the deliberate pu[*rpo*]se of being cut sh[*ort*] . . . .

His mas[*ter*]work reache[*d*] [*pe*]ak in early

plan

E_[____] we

led every kv[*ennik*] s[*tun*]ning [*pens*] live witho[*ut*] moth[*er*]s

not e[*n*]ough b[*u*]ry
beat[*e*]n se[*ver*]ely ey[*e*]

hate to be per[*ceived*] after but
we[*e*]ks fe[*a*]red

It was hell. It hell. not forced to do it. Everything is easier when you're forced to do so, don't you [*think*]? Righteou[*s*] was not en[*ough*]. Keeping safe was not [*enough*].

I am dull no one. But I know suffering. I know what it takes to make it stop.

I still think I went about the wrong [*way*] The suffering of the last experiments and the kvennik carrying them [*was*] pressing. But the suffering of the future . . . I should have gone for his rec[*or*]ds.

I write this now in my own blood, upon my own skin, encased within my o[*wn bone*]. All of this cultured outside my body, in a womb like kvennik's. None of would be po[*ssi*]ble without those damned records.

Even at the end [*of the*] siege —[*the*] planned murder-sui[*cide*] the antidote that 670, lab assistant with better knowledge of than any of us, slipped into siblings' drinks, but not the Doc[*tor's*]—His rotting bo[*dy*] was not enough. should have burned [*it to the*] ground.

I have sealed this within I have no illusions that my own child will be But I can protect them from this. Whether this brutality is hereditary or it was mine.

5. "A Secret" (<30% confidence)
The fifth section—provisionally titled "A Secret" based on the other sections' naming conventions—was too damaged for even piecemeal recreation. Among the phrases predicted with greatest confidence were "difficult to conceive" *(52%)* "my wife" *(47%),* "archive" *(49%),* "genetic" *(41%) and* "to ensure" *(40%).*

Curiously, a fragment of the manuscript appears to have flaked off during necrosis and imprinted on the side of the bone box. It was later recreated with 60% confidence:

we no longer suffer

</Specimen #YY1-340676-A>

Notes:
While **Specimen #YY1-340676***'s obfuscation of places and names ("Dr. _____," "The Observatory at K____") might seem in keeping with Kynish info-suppression, it is not consistent with other Kynish media, which tended to censor wholesale rather than piecemeal. It may therefore have been*

deliberate on the part of the author.

Meanwhile, though the author makes reference to numerous other media describing the Observatory ("Number 348," "his records"), none have been recovered, either at Yor Yan or other Kynish archaeological sites. Assuming that this manuscript does indeed describe a crude precursor to Shell technology—and that the Archive contained other such media and genetic material—this could be a reason for the site's destruction. Partial genotyping of the bone box and flesh paper indicated a genetic link to the precursor of current Shells, lending credence to this hypothesis.

The narrator's brief reference to "viskany" flowers, meanwhile, is intriguing in the context of a bone plaque recovered from the Archive's front wall. The plaque indicated that the director of the Genetic Archive at Yor Yan was Dr. Estek Viskanyas, "noted biologist and contributor to the field of scientific ethics." Several Society members have posited that Dr. Viskanyas could indeed be the "E____ V_____" described in the manuscript's third section. Such plausible connections, while appealing, are unverifiable—even in the context of what the Society found at the hypothesized location of the "Observatory at K______."

A full description of the Society's search methods can be found in under **#YY1-340676-B.** *Succinctly, three rounds of Shells were deployed to Koivin Ras, a famously inaccessible site 167 leagues from Yor Yan. The first two rounds succumbed to delta-stage organ putrefaction—a contagion typical to Kynish sites, though this particular strain was even more virulent than the one at Yor Yan. A third, successfully immunized team of Shells was able to penetrate the site, but was unable to recover any relics—a surprise, as even the most toxic sites often contain traces of human genetic matter. The house, farm, barns, and graveyard—if there ever were any—had been obliterated, and the earth was overgrown with red flowers, each an exact clone of the other.*

J.R. Staples-Ager is currently a PhD student at Yale University, where they research the genetics of chronic pain. They are passionate about science communication and enjoy writing fiction based on real-world biotechnology. Their work can be found in *Luna Station Quarterly* and C.R. Dudley's 2020 science fiction anthology *Vast,* as well as on their blog, bravingthenewworld.wordpress.com.

Once, I returned Tulip, Once I became

CP Nwankwo

once the city sprouted with gods—
seeds whispers, freshly braided with the breaths of the
ancients; tombs cracked impulses like
husks and roots curled from the bones of history. say
once, children built homes in the ribs of
cedars. their colours of laughter carved into a country
bark. once, elders named their dreams
after a tree. for trees do not forget the orders of a lively
hope. once, all things were bright and
beautiful. and eternity was hymnary into the greens of
a monsoon wind. but when the axe is
hungry, ferns unfurl singing dirges to the fractal geo-
metries of empires. only the deeds of
mycelium remembers the threads of hunger in which
she has entertained. does the forest
shrink into memories, if not that the city has lichen a
little normal into ingratitude? take the
crack walls of sycamore and build these heartbreaks
no more, this part where the rain out-
lives the wildness of fire and war. softly, softly the
mercy in the vine would blood over
us. and the borders of dust would come rhythm with
the original poem of god. down the
swollen belly of the earth, the acacia would fold its
leaves like a clasped hand, awaiting
the unction of redemption. the rain would play the
field of angels and the patient hand
would hold a miracle to her pomaces. back to the
prayers that tasted like gunpowder,
locking me like a decked heaven. but the truth is,
I've hurt myself gauzing kindness
out of the neon mouths of an open field. the sight
of me in tender hands of bulrushes.

CP Nwankwo (he/him), SWAN IV, identifies as an apprentice poet. He writes from Port Harcourt, Nigeria. He was recently shortlisted for the Alpine Fellowship Prize for Poetry, 2025. His work is published/forthcoming in *Frontier Poetry*, *Palette Poetry*, *Mizna*, *Magma*, *Heartlines Spec*, *Strange Horizons*, *Reckoning*, *Consequence Forum*, *Lucky Jefferson*, *Rough Cut*, *Another Chicago Magazine*, *Big Score Lit*, *Poetry ColumnNND*, and elsewhere. He tweets @*CPNwankwo*.

Resucitar un río

José Luis Ramirez

No sabía que un río podía declararse clínicamente muerto. Me enteré hace poco, cuando leí que el Atoyac lo estaba y que, desde hacía 30 años, se intentaba rehabilitar. Sin éxito.

No pregunten por qué, pero imagino al río como una persona entrando en camilla a un hospital y los paramédicos gritando a los urgenciólogos: ¡Emergencia Uno! Pero lo cierto es que no es una bella actriz de Bollywood personificando a la Ganga de los Vedas, ni tampoco un atlético hijo de Océano y Tetis. El Atoyac es un pobre diablo apestando a cagada y orines; se convulsiona y suelta espuma por la boca, maldiciendo a todos y cada uno de los bastardos que ha concebido, ladrando como un xoloitzcuintle rabioso. Y son muchos los nombres que grita en esa lengua suya, ininteligible, anterior al protototonaco-tepehua y al protoyuto-nahua.

El río calla de pronto dejando que la sala de urgencias se inunde con el pitido agudo y la línea plana del electrocardiograma, alguien grita: ¡Despejen! y pone las paletas del desfibrilador en su pecho. El cuerpo se arquea un segundo, pienso en la muerte por tétanos. Algún enfermero, sí, varón, le pone un respirador al río y presiona un par de veces la bomba de aire. ¡Despejen! Otra vez y nuevamente descarga. El ECG hace como que regresa, aunque enseguida la línea vuelve a aplanarse.

¿Será que el Atoyac está viendo pasar su vida como en una película?

Una gota de deshielo en la Sierra Nevada, un manantial en la roca, los riachuelos se convierten en afluentes y enseguida un solo cauce, rápidos, caídas de agua, la roca erosionada en gravilla, toda esa energía contenida potencial en la represa de Valsequillo.

O más bien recuerda cómo lo despojaron de cuanto tenía y lo ultrajaron, burlándose además por calentar sus pies descalzos con las aguas tibias que salían del drenaje. Tragar cuanto le pongan en la boca porque el hambre puede siempre más que la dignidad.

El doctor golpea en el pecho, el enfermero aprieta la bomba del respirador, alguien más grita alguna maldición y de la nada surge un latido frágil como la cola de los renacuajos.

No hay más signos vitales.

No hay acto-reflejo al golpear con un martillito en la rodilla ni se dilatan ante la luz las pupilas. Quizás escucha lo que dicen y tal vez esté consciente pero no puede abrir los párpados o responder a los estímulos. ¿Está en coma, catatonia o catalepsia?

Clínicamente muerto se puede malinterpretar, el agua fluye, conserva cierta flora y fauna, aunque 'sano' tampoco lo describe bien, basta mirar los niveles de oxígeno, el PH, las espumas y el color gris taupe, entre marrón y grisáceo . . . .

Los médicos sacan al paciente de urgencias y lo mandan en calidad de desconocido a la Unidad de Cuidados Intensivos. No hay familiar que vele por él. ¿A quién iba a interesarle un viejo inútil? Ciertamente no al gobernador ni al rey de la mezclilla, esos malnacidos que por años violaron a sus hijas, marcando con tinturas y ácidos a sus afluentes más pequeñas. Tampoco a los nietos que hacen negocio trayendo pipas de muy lejos, desecando las lagunas de Totolcingo, El Salado y Alchichica.

Afuera del hospital de especialidades San José llueve, quizás es temporada de huracanes en el Atlántico o haya norte en Veracruz, pero lo cierto es que la tempestad aquí en el valle Puebla-Tlaxcala es más rayos y truenos que otra cosa, ventisca; los granizos golpean con furia, abollan las carrocerías y estrellan los parabrisas, el hielo se derrite en el asfalto, las coladeras se desbordan y de pronto hay lanchas de la Cruz Roja en el Boulevard 5 de Mayo rescatando a los desgraciados que se trepan por las ventanillas al toldo de sus coches.

El desconocido tiene algún espasmo ocasional, no es su única prueba de vida, también el movimiento rápido de los ojos, las ondas beta en el encefalograma, el pulso acelerado. El líquido vital fluye en sus venas y arterias, pero de qué va a servirle si es negro y espeso.

¿Recuerda cuando en 1963 lo confinaron en solitario? Entubando su cauce en el arroyo de Xonaca y el tramo de San Francisco, desde la barranca de Xalpatlac y hasta la 5 Sur esquina con 49 Poniente. Ahí donde todo alrededor se apesta a huevo podrido.

Pero basta de pornomiseria, algún tratamiento habrá equivalente a la hemodiálisis y por los derechos más fundamentales se obligará a las industrias a tratar las aguas residuales, el gobierno tendrá que invertir en un plan trans-sexenal y obligar a la concesionaria de agua potable a invertir en el saneamiento de la cuenca.

Las universidades y la sociedad civil también estarán obligadas por la crisis hídrica, ingenieros ecológicos buscarán métodos para revertir el daño, se impartirá educación ambiental en las escuelas confiando en que las nuevas generaciones serán más conscientes.

Así, el paciente alcanzará algún día a mover un dedo, quizás el meñique izquierdo, aunque nadie lo verá hacerlo, así como tampoco sabrán si escuchaba lo que decían de él mientras estaba en coma y le hacían fisioterapia, que no era nada bueno. Tampoco sabrán cómo es que logró escapar del hospital estando descalzo, con sólo una bata cubriéndole el pecho, pero no las nalgas y literalmente escurriéndosele a los de seguridad.

¿Quién es ese viejo que anda de noche por el boulevard casi desnudo con la lluvia estancada hasta la cintura? ¿Por qué los árboles, palmeras y hasta los postes de luz se mecen rindiéndole pleitesía mientras las intermitentes de los autos abandonados parpadean bajo el agua?

La lluvia le lava las canas largas de la barba y su melena, pegándole la ropa al pecho, cuando el negro de las pupilas del viejo se encienden de un naranja como hierro fundido, el Atoyac junta entonces sus brazos y con toda la fuerza de que es capaz extiende las falanges y en ese gesto de Kame-Hame-Ha cada una de las moléculas que lo conforman se convierten en un tsunami que acarrea basura, lodo y mierda hasta reventar las tuberías que lo contienen, desbordar el cauce y aún explotar la vieja represa en Valsequillo, purificándose en agua nuevamente cristalina que deja entrever las raíces de los juncos y hasta algunos peces entre los guijarros.

Resurrecting a River

José Luis Ramírez

I never knew a river could be in a state of apparent death. I learned about it recently when I read that the Atoyac was declared clinically dead, and for the past 30 years, efforts had been made to rehabilitate it to no avail.

Don't ask why, but I imagine the river as a person being wheeled into a hospital on a stretcher, paramedics shouting at the emergency room doctors: "Code Blue!" But the truth is, she is not a beautiful Bollywood actress personifying the Ganga from the Vedas, nor is he an athletic son of Oceanus and Tethys. The Atoyac is a poor bastard reeking of shit and urine; he convulses and foams at the mouth, cursing every single one of the children he has conceived, barking like a rabid Xoloitzcuintle. And there are many names he screams in his own unintelligible tongue, a language older than Proto-Totonaco-Tepehua and Proto-Yuto-Nahua.

The river suddenly falls silent, letting the emergency room be flooded with the high-pitched beep and the flatline of the electrocardiogram. Someone shouts, "Clear!" and places the defibrillator paddles on his chest. The body arches for a second, as in death by tetanus. A male nurse—yes, a man—puts a respirator on the river's mouth and presses the air pump a couple of times. "Clear!" Again, another shock. The ECG pretends to come back, but soon the line flattens again.

Is the Atoyac watching his life pass by like a movie?

A drop of meltwater in the Sierra Nevada, a spring in the rock, the streams become tributaries, and soon a single channel, rapids, waterfalls, rock eroded into gravel, all that potential energy contained in the Valsequillo dam.

Or rather, he remembers how they stripped him of everything he had and outraged him, mocking him for warming his bare feet with the warm water that came out of the drain. He swallows whatever they put in his mouth because hunger can always overcome dignity.

The doctor pounds on his chest, the male nurse squeezes the respirator pump, someone else shouts a curse, and out of nowhere, a heartbeat emerges, fragile as a tadpole's tail.

There are no more vital signs.

There is no knee-jerk reflex when tapped with a hammer, nor do the pupils dilate in the light. Perhaps he hears what they say, and maybe he is conscious but cannot open his eyelids or respond to stimuli. Is he in a coma, catatonia, or catalepsy?

'Clinically dead' can be misinterpreted. The water flows; it preserves some flora and fauna, although 'healthy' doesn't describe it well either. Just look at the oxygen levels, the pH, the foam, and the taupe color, between brown and grayish . . . .

Doctors take the patient out of emergency room and send him, as John Doe, to the Intensive Care Unit. There is no family member to watch over him. Who would care about an old, useless being? Certainly not the governor or the king of denim, those bastards who for years raped his daughters, marking his smallest tributaries with dyes and acids. Nor the grandchildren who profit by bringing pipes from far away, drying up the lagoons of Totolcingo, El Salado, and Alchichica.

Outside the San José specialty hospital, it rains; it may be due to hurricane season in the Atlantic or perhaps a north wind tempest in Veracruz, but the bottom line is that the storm here in the Puebla-Tlaxcala valley is more lightning and thunder than anything else, a tromba. Hailstones fall furiously, denting car bodies and shattering windshields; ice melts on the asphalt, drains overflow, and suddenly Red Cross boats appear on 5 de Mayo Boulevard rescuing the unfortunate who climb onto the roofs of their cars through the windows.

The stranger has an occasional spasm; it's not his only proof of life, as there is also the rapid movement of his eyes, the beta waves on the electroencephalogram, the accelerated pulse. The vital fluid flows through his veins and arteries, but what good will it do if it is black and thick?

Does he remember when, in 1963, he was confined in solitary? Tubed and channeled at the Xonaca stream and the San Francisco section, from the Xalpatlac ravine to the corner of 5 Sur and 49 Poniente? There, where everything around stinks of rotten eggs.

Enough with the misery porn! Some treatment will be equivalent to hemodialysis, and, for the most fundamental rights, industries will be forced to treat wastewater. The government will have to invest in a trans-sexennial plan and mandate the drinking water concessionaire to contribute to basin sanitation.

Universities and civil society will also be forced to act by the water crisis; ecological engineers will seek methods to reverse the damage, and environmental education will be taught in schools, entrusting that the new generations will be more aware.

Thus, the patient will one day be able to move a finger, perhaps his left pinky, although no one will see him do it, just as they will not know if he was listening to what they were saying about him while he was in a coma and they were doing physiotherapy—words that were not kind. Nor will they know how he managed to escape from the hospital barefoot, with only a gown covering his chest but not his buttocks, and literally 'slipping' away from security guys.

Who is that old man walking at night down the boulevard, almost naked, with the rainwater up to his waist? Why do the trees, palm trees, and even the light poles sway, paying homage to him while the turn signals of abandoned cars blink under the water?

Rain washes the long gray hair from his beard and his mane, sticking his clothes to his chest. Then the black of the old man's pupils lights up orange like molten iron, the Atoyac brings his arms together and, with all his might, extends his fingers. In that gesture of Kame-Hame-Ha, each molecule in his body becomes a tsunami that carries garbage, mud, and filth until it bursts the pipes that contain him, overflows the riverbed, and even ruptures the old Valsequillo dam, purifying itself in water that becomes crystal clear again, revealing the roots of the reeds and even some fish among the pebbles.

José Luis Ramírez (Puebla, MX. 1974) is an Industrial Engineer in Electronics and completed a master's degree in Computer Science. He has been published in various anthologies, as well as in several magazines and fanzines. He won the National Prize for Fantastic and Science Fiction Short Story in 1998 with the short story 'Hielo.'

Agujero Negro

Luis Rafael Moya

en memoria de todos los lenguajes perdidos y por perderse

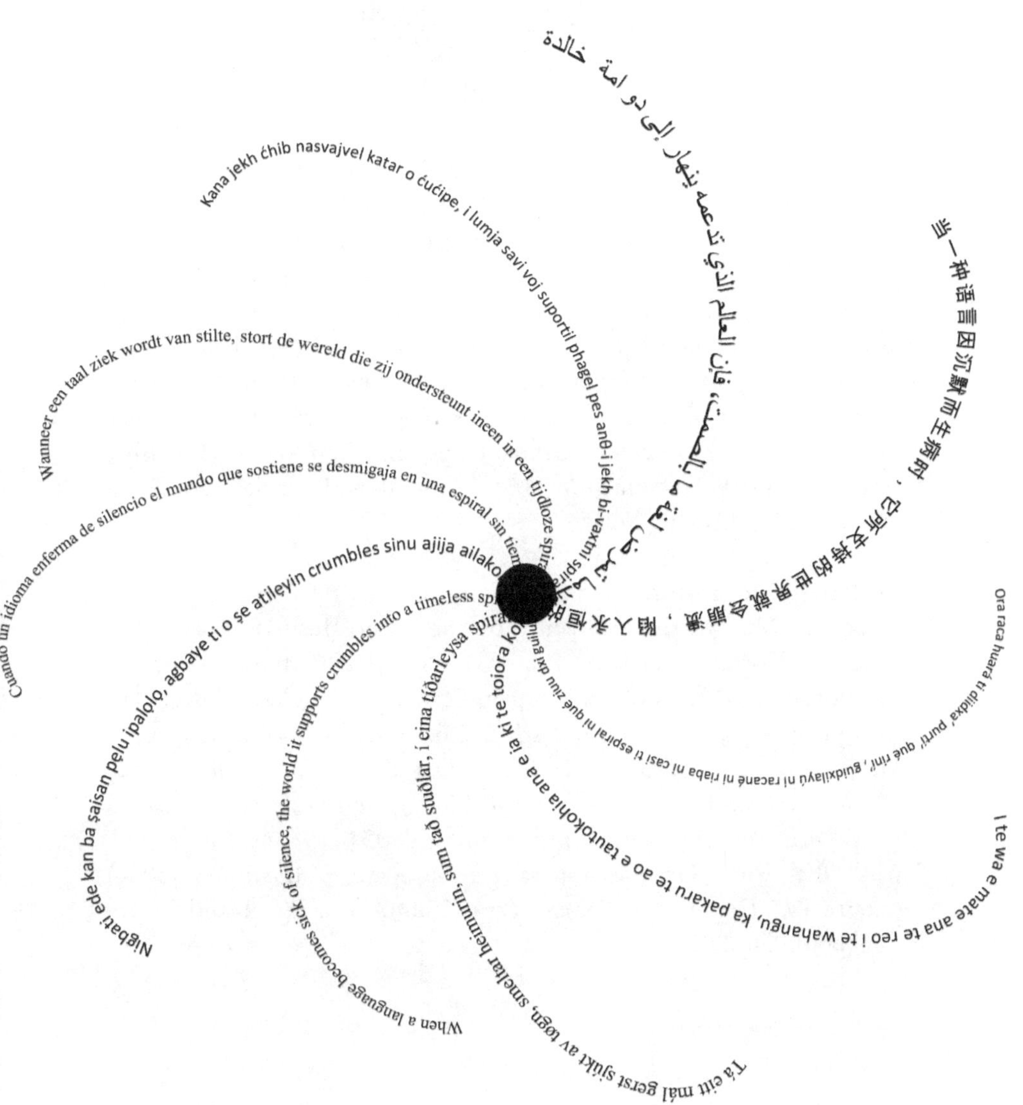

Luis. Rafael. Moya. Nacido en domingo del año 1997, mes de Mayo, Carúpano. Fue, o es: Abogado. Lector de cartas. Vendedor de seguros. Traductor. Escritor de artículos. Editor. Síndico procurador. Bartender. Carnicero. Recepcionista. Vendedor de galletas. Escapista. Tutor de niños con discapacidad. Apareció en: *Postpoesía I, II* y *III* (2023), *Antología incendiaria* (2023), *micro poemas para microondas* (2023), *Treinta Tristes Tautogramas* (2023), *¡K.O. la antología más cota del mundo!* (2023), *Torneo de poemas tácticos* (2024), *Diciembre es el segundo mes más cruel* (2024), *No me dejes en visto* (2024), el cuento "Grandes esperanzas" en *Revista Alborismos* (2024), "Voltaire IV" *Diario de los Andes Perú* (2024), Feria del libro digital de New York y Lisboa (2023).

Luis. Rafael. Moya. Born on a Sunday in the year 1997, month of May, Carúpano. Was, or is: Lawyer. Fortune teller. Insurance salesman. Translator. Writer of articles. Editor. Union rep. Bartender. Butcher. Receptionist. Seller of cookies. Escapist. Teacher of disabled children. Has appeared in: *Postpoesía I, II,* and *III* (2023), *Antología incendiaria* (2023), *micro poemas para microondas* (2023), *Treinta Tristes Tautogramas* (2023), *¡K.O. la antología más cota del mundo!* (2023), *Torneo de poemas tácticos* (2024), *Diciembre es el segundo mes más cruel* (2024), *No me dejes en visto* (2024), the story "Grandes esperanzas" in *Revista Alborismos* (2024), "Voltaire IV" *Diario de los Andes Perú* (2024), New York and Lisbon digital book fair (2023).

Point Wolf

Geneva Toland

WOLF POINT[1]

The Lewis and Clark Expedition passed by here, westward bound, in May 1805. Fur trappers and traders followed them a few years later. Steamboats began making it from St. Louis up the Missouri as far as Fort Benton in the early 1860s. Wolf Point was the halfway point between Bismarck and Fort Benton. Wood choppers supplied cord wood for boats stopping to refuel. The American Fur Company packet *Chippewa* blew up and sank not far from here in 1861. A deck hand tapped a barrel of alcohol by candle light. The fumes, the candle and the 25 kegs of black powder did the rest. Fortunately, no lives were lost in the disaster.

Wolf Point originated as a sub-agency and trading post for the Fort Peck Reservation in 1879. The place was named when trappers killed several hundred wolves one winter and stacked their frozen carcasses next to the river, where they were observed by men heading upriver on a steamboat. The name Wolf Point stuck and no one there has been bothered by a wolf at the door since then.

POINT WOLF

Several hundred wolves traded songs one winter, harmonizing upriver under frozen black fumes. The river was a halfway point between men and lives lost, steamboats stacked like carcasses upon each other. The 25 remaining fur trappers and traders followed the wolves to a place named woods, for that is what they were and there was no bother

1. Text of a historical marker erected at Wolf Point, Roosevelt County, Montana by the Montana Department of Transportation

to name things anymore. The men carried candles in their hands to refuel the fires the wolves had kept burning for them. Lewis and Clark slicked like strange words on their tongues, when the wolves asked for the sub-agency responsible for the westward disaster. The trappers stuck out their palms for the wolves to lick the keg powder off. No one returned to the Company. No one supplied the Fort. Fortunately, the river stuck its course and soon the whole Point traded light for depth. The wolves barreled around the last standing door, observing the original agreement to which they were bound to sing the early years backwards. The men sunk to their knees and no one has bothered the wolves since then.

The Hot Spring Post-Pinkerton

Geneva Toland

PINKERTON HOT SPRINGS[1]

Even though this land was Ute territory, the upper Animas River Valley was first settled by prospectors in the spring of 1860. Charles Baker, returning from the mines north of Silverton, established "Old Animas City" and built the first bridge across the Animas River. The community lasted less than a year before it was abandoned. During the summer of 1875, James Harvey Pinkerton settled in the area now known as Pinkerton Hot Springs. He raised dairy cows with his wife, three sons, and four daughters. Throughout the year they produced and sold dairy products in mining camps in the San Juan Mountains. In the spring of 1876 they sold 116 pounds of butter for a dollar a pound to the miners north of Silverton.

THE HOT SPRING POST-PINKERTON

Even though, the community abandoned the land. Even though, the cows and prospectors produced and sold the mountains. Even though, Charles Baker lasted less than a summer in the Valley and produced no wife. Even though, the butter fattened the sons on all the miners' daughters. Even though a dollar couldn't settle the spring and the area known as the River of lost mining camps pounded the bridge until it broke and fell through. Even though, Pinkerton took his wife and his 116 cows to the fat river and drowned. Even though, the north blew in 1876 snowstorms and blew out 1875 hot summers. Even though, the community abandoned the land and abandoned the land and abandoned the land. Even though, this territory was first and now Ute land. Even now, this old, old land. Even now.

---

1. Text of a historical marker erected near Durango in La Plata County, Colorado by the Colorado Department of Transportation—San Juan Skyway

Geneva Toland is a writer, farmer, naturalist, and educator currently working towards her MFA in Poetry at the Institute for American Indian Arts. Her writing has appeared in *Southern Humanities Review, Camas, humana obscura,* and *West Trade Review*, among others. She is also a poetry editor at Terrain and Chapter House Journal. She feels humbled to live in the juniper and piñon pine foothills of the La Plata mountains, homelands of the Ute, Diné and Puebloan peoples. See her other offerings at www.genevatoland.com.

To Stand, You Must Be Rooted

Verdell Walker

"What should we bring Pawpaw for dinner?" I asked Mama.

Her bronze urn rested in the passenger's seat, secured by the seat belt. Her ghost sat in the backseat, wearing the green skirt suit I'd buried her in, a thin blue aura haloing her body.

We were driving from Birmingham to Pawpaw's farm in Sweetcreek. The high-rises and billboards gradually surrendered to fields of soybeans, corn, and cotton. The heat tested the limits of my Corolla's air conditioning, and its tires were barely a match for the red dirt backroads. Roadside joints selling BBQ and fried fish plates cropped up like mushrooms. Mama narrowed her eyes in the rearview mirror. I could almost hear her suck her teeth, deriding them as country and low class.

"Ribs, I think," I murmured to myself.

An hour later, I pulled into the farmhouse's driveway with two rib plates and four suitcases. The single story house was white with green shutters and a black roof, set back from the road and fronted by a yard filled with pink azaleas and blue hydrangeas. In the far distance stood greenhouses and rows of garden boxes bursting with herbs. Pawpaw never had any powers to speak of, but he certainly had a green thumb, which is its own kind of magic if you ask me.

He sat on the porch, wearing a starched white shirt, pressed jeans, and a pristine Stetson. Gold front tooth gleaming, he grinned as I ran up the porch steps and into his waiting arms.

"Hey there, Lil' Partner."

"Hey there, Big Partner."

Pawpaw was thinner than I remembered, and I didn't miss the way he'd risen stiffly from his chair. But he still smelled the same: tobacco, mint, and Irish Spring.

He wouldn't let me carry in my luggage, so while he brought my suitcases up to Mama's childhood bedroom, I took her urn and our dinner into the kitchen. It was clean and bright as always, smelling faintly of lemon. I half-expected Granma to be there, kneading biscuits or frying chicken. But she wasn't, and neither was her ghost.

"Did you finish Granma's headstone?" I asked Pawpaw when he came in.

"Finally found that doggone recipe," Pawpaw chuckled.

"Thelma had it stuffed in a shoebox. Raymond finished the engraving last month." He looked down at the checkerboard tile floor. "Everything still feels strange without her."

Granma had died the year before, Mama three years before her. You'd think I would've been a pro at grief and loss, but no such luck.

"Can I go see her?" I asked. The family cemetery was a short drive away.

"Another time, Monica. You should get some rest." Pawpaw only used my name when he made gentle "suggestions". He nodded at Mama's urn. "We can lay Gertrude to rest later, too."

Mama had hated her name, insisting on being called Trudy by everyone. "When the cancer came back, she told me she wanted her ashes spread next to Granma's grave whenever she died."

I watched him absorb this information. He couldn't have been more surprised than I'd been by Mama's request. She and Granma had had a difficult relationship. A difficult relationship with a mother was one of the few things I'd had in common with Trudy.

"Well, I'm gonna respect my baby's wishes. And I'm gonna do it proper," Pawpaw said finally. "But today I gotta make some deliveries."

Mama stood in the corner, thin fingers resting on her collarbone, a pained look on her face.

"And go see the developer," I added.

"He's offering twenty million now," Pawpaw said, rubbing his jaw.

I whistled. "Wow . . . wow."

"Yeah, I know."

I set the BBQ plates in the oven for dinner. Neither Pawpaw nor Granma had ever approved of microwaves. Didn't trust them. "I'm coming with you."

"Ain't you tired?"

I kissed his cheek, his skin wrinkled like crepe paper. "Yes, but I like to watch you work. And I want to meet this man for myself."

Over his shoulder, Mama turned and disappeared. A part of me wanted to tell Pawpaw I'd been seeing her for weeks, but I kept silent. He had enough to worry about.

I helped Pawpaw load his truck with the orders. As a girl, Mama had painted the farm's name and tagline on the truck's doors: *Sweetcreek Farms. Fine Herbs & Plants.* Granma had drawn a picture of the High John the Conqueror root our farm was known for. Seeing it always made me chuckle; it made the farm seem downright ordinary. For over a century, our family had supplied root workers and other magical practitioners across the South and beyond with the herbs and plants they needed for their spells, rituals, and potions.

As we bounced along the dirt backroads, Pawpaw quizzed me about the uses of the plants packaged in the purple sachets Granma had sewn. As I answered each one correctly, a ghost of a smile tugged at Pawpaw's lips. I'd been studying, so I could be useful to him. There'd been little else to do in the six months since I'd been laid off. He didn't say so, but I could tell he was pleased with my knowledge. He and Granma had feared it would die with Mama, who'd been determined to put as much physical and emotional distance as possible between herself and the family legacy. Not just growing the plants, but serving the people who used them and those who wanted someone to conjure on their behalf.

"It's always something with these Negroes," Mama groused to me once when I was eight. We were at Sweetcreek for a rare Christmas visit, watching Granma give mojo bags, amulets, and teas to people looking for help with all sorts of problems while our dinner cooled. "She got more time for them than for her own family."

A stern look from Pawpaw had quieted Mama's complaints but that was the first time I'd noticed the unspoken tension between her and Granma. And it was the last time Mama had bothered to hide her displeasure with our life from me.

❧

The delivery list had forty names. These were some of Pawpaw's longstanding, most valued customers, women who bought from him in bulk. There were grandmothers with lined, brown faces and wrinkled hands and Millennials with dreadlocks, headwraps, and nose rings. He made a point to chat with each of them, asking after their families and health. Only at the end of these conversations did he deftly inquire about what magic they expected to work in the coming weeks and months, sussing out what they'd need for future orders, which I dutifully recorded in a small notebook.

My heart leapt when we got to Miss Eulalie, Miss Pearl, and Miss Henrietta, three of Granma's closest friends. I remembered them from childhood summers, when Mama sent me down South so she could work overtime without guilt and fraternize with her boyfriends. They were consummate conjure women, renowned for their skills and potions just as Granma had been. They hadn't changed a bit: Eulalie, in leopard leggings with long red acrylics, trailed by three cats; Pearl in her pressed usher's uniform and immaculate steel-gray chignon; and Henrietta in her overalls and sturdy work boots, motor oil and grease under her nails. They exclaimed over me, pressing vials of oils and tinctures into my hands, which they promised would bring me luck, prosperity, and a fertile womb. I didn't want kids but the mentions of fertility didn't make me feel nearly as awkward as their questions about my craft. Pawpaw looked at his feet whenever this came up.

"I haven't had time for spellwork lately," was my standard reply before changing the subject. They didn't need to know I could barely summon a candle flame these days, or that Mama's ghost appeared whenever she wanted rather than from my summons, nor could I banish her when her presence threatened to suffocate me.

But they told us something that made a knot of dread settle in my stomach like a coiled snake—Sweetcreek's produce was changing. Henrietta had noticed that some of her spells didn't last as long as they used to. Eulalie was forced to use twice as much black snake root now in her protection charms. Pearl's last batch of candles had burned with acrid, black smoke that curled in unnatural spirals.

It wasn't just them. A few of the older women, those who'd been using the farm's herbs for years, who could observe the changes between then and now, told us similar things.

"How long has this been going on?" I asked Pawpaw back in the truck.

His work-gnarled hands tightened on the steering wheel. "A few years. Was hard to notice at first. Land seems angry."

I listened as Pawpaw described the upheaval at Sweetcreek and the farms of his friends. Stronger, more destructive hurricanes tore through fields, burning summers scorched tender plants, and pests never seen before chewed through crops before they could flourish.

"Sounds like climate change. It must be impacting the potency of the herbs and plants." I shook my head, furious and powerless, at the massive forces making his hard job even harder.

"That's what the news say. I don't doubt it, though I don't know too much science myself. But I don't think that's all."

"What else could it be?"

Pawpaw rubbed his jaw. "Something broke when Gertrude left. Thelma's magic wasn't the same after that. That wasn't noticeable at first, either. But spells she used to be able to work with her eyes closed, she could barely do them by the end."

I kept my eyes on the road. Mama took me away from Sweetcreek when I was five, tired of being judged for having a baby out of wedlock, tired of living under Granma's roof.

"Mama never used her magic much besides little stuff like healing baths and burning sage to purify our apartment," I said quietly. "I never thought anything of it till I saw what Granma could do. Maybe Mama couldn't do more than that."

Pawpaw nodded. "Maybe not. Magic don't run in men, you know, so I couldn't tell you."

"Well, we both know I'm a failure in that arena, so I couldn't tell you either." I laughed ruefully. "A failure in most arenas lately."

"Don't ever say that," Pawpaw snapped. He pulled over and fixed me with a hard look. "Stop listening to the lies the Devil tell."

Pawpaw was such a calm, easygoing man. I was taken aback by his vehemence, his fierce belief in my worth. I nodded, swallowing hard and weaving my fingers with his. He patted my hand, kissed it.

I rested my head on his shoulder. "I should've come home sooner."

"You're here now."

We sat in silence in the truck, Pawpaw slumped against his seat. After a few minutes he spoke again. "Since Thelma died, a lot of the ladies come round and help me bless the soil." He swiped a hand over his face. "It helps, but the land still seems upset. Agitated. Out of balance."

I squeezed his knee. He could've been talking about me.

The next day, Pawpaw and I headed to Langston, the closest thing to a city near Sweetcreek, to meet the developer. I expected Ryan Cutler to be a standard issue good ol' boy, but he was actually a standard issue finance bro, like the ones who'd fired just about everybody at my old job. He had a pale, forgettable face, with watery blue eyes and wheat-colored hair.

"Good to see you, Eugene!" Ryan said, extending a hand to Pawpaw.

"Mr. Hayes," I corrected him, stepping slightly in front of Pawpaw and intercepting the handshake. "And I'm Ms. Monica Hayes, his granddaughter."

Ryan's fingers were puffy and his palm was moist. I hid my disgust as I pumped his hand with more force than was necessary. He looked flustered as I held his gaze before sitting in one of the chairs at the gleaming glass table in his office. Pawpaw shot me a look of proud gratitude as he removed his hat and sat beside me. I knew he'd never be comfortable correcting a white man, even if it was to insist on respect.

I'm here now, Pawpaw.

"My grandfather told me about your offer, but I'd like to hear it from the horse's mouth."

Ryan looked at Pawpaw, who looked back at him without saying a word.

"Ms. Hayes, I've made your grandfather a substantial offer for his land. I'm assembling several properties for warehouse development. My goal is to transform Sweetcreek into a logistics hub—it'll bring jobs and much needed economic growth to the area."

I'd heard this spiel before. "Why should he sell to you? Our land has been in our family for generations."

Again, Ryan cut his eye to Pawpaw. Again, Pawpaw remained silent.

Ryan exhaled loudly. "Ma'am, your family has done an incredible job. And you've got a nice niche with that woo-woo stuff. You're not at the mercy of the market in the same way commodity farmers are."

I bared my teeth at him in an imitation of a smile. "Woo-woo stuff?"

Chuckling, Ryan wiggled his fingers. "Great idea. All you're missing is crystals. My niece loves crystals, has a shelf full of them."

Pawpaw let out a frayed huff, thumbing the edge of his Stetson.

Ryan barreled on, oblivious. "But I'm sure you know farming is a hell of a lot of work. Your grandpa takes on a ton of risk to not make a lot of money. The interest on the money I'm offering is more than he'd make in a good year. I'm giving him a very attractive way out."

Nothing Ryan said was wrong. I was certain a spreadsheet somewhere on his blocky Thinkpad laid it out in black and white, some complex financial model that calculated our land's value down to the penny, spitting out the number that would make Ryan a tidy profit and make an old man go away quietly.

But none of that accounted for the magic in the soil, the power that produced some of the most coveted and revered magical flora in the world. Or at least, it had.

Ryan twirled his wedding band, looking at the gold ring instead of me. "These warehouses are tens of thousands of square feet. They need a ton of land. I've made offers to other farmers around here."

Pawpaw spoke for the first time. "Twenty of them."

Surprise flickered across Ryan's face before he smothered it. "Many of them are keen to sell for all the reasons we've discussed, but your holdings are the anchor."

I frowned. "What does that mean?"

"It means the development falls apart without your land, because the parcel won't be big enough for the warehouse complex. If Mr. Hayes doesn't sell, then the other farmers won't get their money."

The Saturday morning after our meeting with Cutler, the other farmers came by to beg, cajole, and threaten Pawpaw into selling his land. He patiently listened to everyone, telling them he was still thinking and praying on his decision. Logically, I knew those farmers were also struggling with ailing land and shrinking bank accounts. But in my heart I resented them for descending on Pawpaw like hungry locusts devouring his peace. I'd had enough; I needed to get out of the house before I punched someone.

The screen door banged behind me as I bounded down the porch steps, my feet carrying me to the fields. The sun bore down hard as I meandered along the packed dirt path winding through the rows and rows of plants nestled in moist black soil in cedar garden boxes Pawpaw had built by hand. A ring of greenhouses protecting the more delicate, heat-sensitive plants like bayberry surrounded the fields, their panes glinting in the sun. The air smelled sharp and medicinal in some areas, then sweet, earthy, and musky in others. All was quiet except for the buzz of bees, the low hum of cicadas, and the dirt crunching under my shoes. My hands grazed the tall, lance-shaped leaves of the Queen Elizabeth root, rubbed the waxy, viridian leaves of rue growing in a lacy pattern, stroked the rough, ropey bundles of angelica root drying on posts.

"Monica!"

I turned to see Miss Henrietta loping toward me, smiling wide under a straw hat and carrying a large paper bag. "Brought you and Eugene some lunch!"

Henrietta was a big woman, tall and powerfully built. She intimidated a lot of people, but I knew her as the dispenser of some of the world's best hugs. Once she turned me loose, I peered inside the bag, greeted by the heavenly scent of two pork sandwiches wrapped in grease-stained brown paper and a dozen tea cakes.

"You didn't have to do this!"

"No, but I wanted to," she replied, patting my cheek with her calloused hand. "Why you out here?"

I ignored her question, letting another that had been simmering leap out instead. "Will you make me a mojo bag?"

Confusion flickered across Henrietta's face. "What kind?"

I shuffled my feet. "Prosperity. Money. Finding a new job."

She glanced at Pawpaw on the porch, trying to shake a departing farmer's hand. The man swatted his palm aside and stormed off. Word of Cutler's offer had traveled fast, but she didn't pry.

"Alright. Let's go to Thelma's workshop."

Pawpaw still kept the workshop tidy. Dried bundles of herbs hung from the rafters. Mason jars lined the shelves, filled with roots, powders, and stones, their names written in Sharpie in Granma's neat hand on masking tape labels. A long wooden table in the center of the room was covered with tools—knives and spoons, a mortar and pestle, scissors, several chipped bowls, a small cauldron, and a brazier. A wicker basket filled with old fabric pouches sat underneath.

Mama had appeared again, frowning at Henrietta as she scanned the shelves for the necessary ingredients. I ignored her, turning on two ceiling fans that pushed the hot air around. Henrietta deposited an armful of jars, herbs, and roots on the table. Her nimble hands moved with precision over the plants and tools.

"Alfalfa," she said, crumbling a handful of dried leaves in her palm. They released a faint, grassy scent as they rained into a bowl. "It keeps money steady in your house."

To draw money and prosperity to me, she added powdered sassafras and bayberry bark. Then cinnamon, "to make that money come quick". High John was next. She held the dark, knobby pods reverently before grinding them up, her brawny forearm working the pestle. As she worked, she whispered prayers for my prosperity over the ingredients. Mama watched from the corner, her arms folded over her chest.

"Mama didn't like you."

As soon as the words escaped my lips, I snapped my mouth shut. Henrietta stopped grinding. *What the hell possessed me to admit that?*

Before I could apologize, Henrietta said, "I didn't like her either. Biggety self."

Mama looked at me expectantly; I suppose waiting for me to defend her. Instead I asked, "Why do you say that?"

"She was ashamed of where she come from," Henrietta answered as she resumed grinding. "Ashamed of the work that kept her fed and helped poor folks around here that didn't have nothing but prayer and Thelma."

I thought of all the times I'd heard Mama disparage Sweetcreek. Poverty had been her greatest fear. She saw how hard Pawpaw and Granma worked and yet how precarious things could still be. To her, root work was something poor people used because they didn't have anything better. It wasn't power, it was the legacy of slaves and sharecroppers—the weak and abused, in her mind.

"She always pushed me to excel in school. She didn't want me to end up like her—selling nice things she couldn't afford to rich people, working long hours but still needing food stamps."

"Well, maybe it wouldn't have come to that if she hadn't run off and took you with her."

No matter how well I'd done in school and how far I'd risen professionally, it never felt like enough for Mama. And a fat lot of good it had done me in the end, when all my achievement and self-worth had been ripped away in a five minute Zoom with HR. "Maybe," I said.

Henrietta shook her head. "Gertrude broke Thelma's heart. She turned her back on who she was. How can you stand if you ain't rooted?"

Mama's face was devoid of expression except for the smoldering look in her eyes.

"Go get a bag from the basket, baby. A green one."

I did as Henrietta asked. When I returned to the table, Mama was gone. I held the small bag open and Henrietta carefully poured in the mojo mixture then tied it shut with gold string. She lit a bit of incense in the brazier, the warm, spicy scent filling the room. Passing the bag through the smoke, Henrietta murmured words too soft for me to catch. Finally, she held the bag to her lips, exhaling a long huff of air into it, before handing it over to me.

"What was that for?"

"I breathed life into it," she said, her eyes meeting mine. "You gotta feed the bag once a month to keep the energy strong. I hold it in my hand on a full moon and speak my intentions over it again. But your gut will tell you what *you* need to do."

I snorted. "You're giving me too much credit."

Henrietta cupped my cheek. "What you need is already in you, baby. Me, Pearl, and Eulalie will help you find it."

"You know how the land got power?"

I turned away from Vanna White on the TV to look at Pawpaw. "Mama told me the land woke up when my great-grandmother killed a man."

"Verlean. To save her husband Elijah's life. And it was two men. White men, no less."

"*Lord*. How did she get away with that?"

"No body, no problem, I guess." Pawpaw's lips formed a smug curve. "And even the white folks back then knew the women in this family were strong root workers, even if they didn't understand or believe in conjure."

Now *that* was new information to me. "Why was Elijah attacked?"

Pawpaw's face hardened. "A Black family owning any land, even hardscrabble land . . . well, to a lot white folks in Sweetcreek that wasn't to be borne. Uppity nigger had to be dealt with."

Bile rose in my throat. "What exactly happened?"

"It's fuzzy. Verlean and Elijah didn't like to talk about it, as you might expect. But what's important is that the land came to Verlean's defense, *came alive*. After that, everything grown in this soil made the best magic you could get." He took my hands in his own, his weathered brown fingers rubbing my much softer ones. "And the hands that grew those plants did too."

I shifted uncomfortably as a sharp twinge of unease gripped my heart and squeezed. "And it can again. Henrietta said she and the other ladies would teach me—"

Pawpaw cut me off. "I'm selling, Lil' Partner."

Without thinking, I shot up, nearly toppling over because my legs had gone to sleep. "You can't! You can't let these people bully you into giving all this away! You've worked too hard!"

Pawpaw looked up at me, weary. "Ain't nobody bullying me, baby. I'm tired. And the land is, too. I feel it every time I go to the fields."

I couldn't argue with him, with the defeated cast of his shoulders, with the exhaustion carving every line in his face. Because even in the short time I'd been there, I could also feel the energy in the land dimming with each passing day, probably even more keenly than Pawpaw.

"What about me?" I whimpered. "I wanted this to be my home."

Pawpaw held my hand to his heart. "I was thinking of you when I decided. I'll have enough money to make sure you're taken care of. And wherever I am, you got a home."

I couldn't get Verlean off my mind or Pawpaw's words: *the land came to her defense*. How? And, I thought bitterly, why wasn't it rising to our defense now?

The day after Pawpaw told me of his decision, the land decided to answer the first question.

I was weeding herb beds when Elijah ran past me. I recognized him from old family photos. He looked over his shoulder at me, eyes wide with terror. For a moment, I thought I'd finally lost my mind. But then the thunder of hooves made the ground shake underneath me. Two men on horseback streaked by, one of them striking Elijah in the head with a baton. Elijah crumpled to the dirt, bleeding from the temple. The other man dismounted and began to beat Elijah. The vision was muffled; the men's shouts and Elijah's screams sounded like they were underwater. I was heartily glad. I didn't need to hear the meaty smacks of fists on flesh. I squeezed my eyes shut, my breath coming in frantic punches.

When I cracked open an eye, hoping desperately for the vision to be gone, Verlean was there. She launched herself at Elijah's attacker but he flung her aside like a dirty rag and kicked her in the stomach. Elijah crawled over, trying to shield his wife from the blows.

Suddenly, a pulse of magic rocked the earth. Verlean's eyes

clouded over in cataracts. She thrust out her hand and the two men flew backward, one falling off his rearing horse, the other hitting a tree. Verlean staggered to her feet and raised her hands to the sky. Darkness rolled over the land. Then she slammed her palms against the dirt and the pulse flared again. Even outside the vision, I felt it in my body. The trees, the grass, the flowers, and all the other plants grew uncontrollably as the ground opened up and devoured Elijah's attackers, sucking them down in a maelstrom of dirt and rocks. Another pulse knocked me off my feet. I lay there in the dirt for what seemed like hours, sweating and gulping down air. When I lifted my head, the vision had receded.

"That was horrible," I croaked out. "Why did you show me that?"

The trilling of the cicadas was the only response I got.

It was a harvest day—and night. The red sun dipped toward the horizon but the heat wasn't giving up without a fight. Rivulets of sweat streaked down my back and between my breasts, soaking the mojo bag pinned to my sports bra. The waxing moon would soon be visible, time for us to gather the bay laurel, rue, and High John. We'd pick well into the night. Some of Pawpaw's fellow deacons were stationed at the edge of the fields, frying catfish in vats of oil to slap on white bread with pickles and mustard for dinner.

Pawpaw was waiting for Cutler to draw up the paperwork before telling anyone of his decision. This would be one of the final harvests.

I walked through the rows of garden boxes, checking for leaves nibbled by pests and testing the soil moisture. For the dry plants, of which there were many, I summoned tiny rainclouds to water them. The clouds were a step above pathetic, but they got the job done if I concentrated hard enough. I had just enough magic to keep the phalanx of mosquitoes from biting, but they still swarmed.

A small army of teenagers making a few extra dollars were harvesting other herbs by hand, cutting and tying them into bundles. These would go into the drying houses for inspection, processing, and packaging. The inspection was the important part, testing the energy, potency, and spiritual qualities of the plants before they were sold—this was once Granma's job. Henrietta, Pearl, and Eulalie were doing it now.

Pawpaw paid them in herbs and roots, but I suspected their concern for him and enduring love for Granma were the greater motivators.

As I approached the drying house, I could hear Eulalie through the open door, telling bawdy stories about old lovers that made Henrietta guffaw and Pearl chide her good-naturedly. I'd told no one of my vision, and I yearned for their company to put it behind me. But when I stepped inside, the smile died on my face.

Granma stood in their midst, wearing a red dress dotted with tiny white flowers, smiling beatifically at me.

Eulalie looked up from burning sage. "What's wrong, baby?"

I opened my mouth, but no sound came out. The love shining in Granma's eyes hit me like an arrow to the chest.

"What do you see?" Henrietta asked knowingly. "*Who* do you see?"

"Granma," I whispered.

Pearl gasped. The women looked at each other, then at me.

"Can y'all see her?" I asked them, desperate.

"No," Henrietta said gently. "But she ain't here for us."

They arrayed themselves around me, placing gentle hands on my shoulders and arms.

"I've missed you so much," I said to Granma. "There's so much I need to talk to you about. Pawpaw and I . . . everything is slipping away . . . ."

Granma walked toward me. I felt cold, the hairs on my arms lifting. She raised her hand to my face, her fingers hovering near my cheek. Then she moved to the door, motioning for me to come along. She looked out across the fields, her expression worried. I followed her gaze and saw Pawpaw standing near the angelica root. He turned and looked right at us.

"Can he see you too?"

Pawpaw took one step forward, two, three. Then he clutched his chest, his face screwing up tight, and dropped to his knees in the dirt.

~

"If you don't go home and get some sleep, you'll be in here next," the nurse said.

I sat by Pawpaw's bedside, watching his chest rise and fall in his sleep. The heart monitor beeped steadily, each ping a reminder of how close I'd come to losing him. The harsh fluorescent lights cast shadows across his face, and his hands rested limply against the crisp white sheets. He wore a mojo bag around his neck filled with healing herbs, made by Miss Eulalie. I trusted it as much as the meds the doctors had given him.

"He's an old man, isn't he?" I said.

The nurse squeezed my shoulder and handed me a cup of water. I drank it, more to ease the tightness in my throat than from thirst. My face was tight from the salt of dried tears. I kissed Pawpaw's forehead and whispered, "I'll be back tomorrow."

His face looked peaceful. It enraged me that it'd taken a goddamn heart attack for my poor grandfather to finally get some rest.

Restless, I drove around town for a while before an impulse became a conviction. I stopped at the farmhouse and got Mama's urn then headed to our cemetery. Pale moonlight filtered through the old oaks and pines, illuminating weathered headstones and patches of herbs growing among the graves. Here was where we grew our family stores of magical herbs, close to the bones of our loved ones. I walked to Granma's grave, an empty space next to it clearly meant for Pawpaw. A shudder traveled through my body.

I stroked Granma's polished headstone. Underneath her name, life dates, and 1 Corinthians 15:55 was the recipe for her famous caramel cake, the one she'd refused to share in life. At the end it said, "Hope y'all happy now. Love, Thelma."

Screams erupted around me—wild, guttural, strangled keening. It took my brain a minute to process that they were coming from me.

My throat raw and nose running, I ripped the lid off Mama's urn. "You don't deserve this, but maybe this will make you leave me the hell alone."

I dumped her ashes beside Granma. Guilt over not waiting for Pawpaw pecked me with a sharp beak but I ignored it. When the urn was empty, I flung it away from me. It sailed through the air and hit a tree festooned with Spanish moss with a metallic thunk.

Spent from rage and despair, I sank to the ground. Suddenly, the humid air grew colder by several degrees. Two bare brown feet appeared before me. My gaze traveled up a gray homespun dress before settling on a delicately pretty face topped with a red headscarf.

Verlean.

I reached out to touch her but of course my hand passed through her, as if through mist.

"Can you help me?" I pleaded. "Can you wake the land up again?"

She shook her head no, pointed at me.

I punched the grass. "My magic is dying, just like our land. *I* can't do anything!"

Verlean licked her lips, looked over my shoulder. Granma stood behind me. And beside her was Mama.

"What the hell do *you* want?" I snarled. "You started this in the first place. This is all your fault!"

To my undying shock, Mama nodded. *But I'm here now*, she mouthed.

Tears sprang to my eyes again, unbidden. "It's too late. Pawpaw is selling. We're gonna lose everything."

Verlean knelt, her hand hovering over the grass covering Granma's grave and Mama's ashes. Her eyes bore into mine, and snatches from my vision of her placing her palms on the ground and the land bursting to life flitted through my mind. Verlean nodded, like she could see the memories. Granma and Mama stood on my left and right, their palms raised upward.

Tentatively, I placed my hands on the soil, my fingers sinking into it, dirt collecting under my nails.

And then I felt it—the power.

It surged up through my palms, a crackling force vibrating through my bones. Magic coursed through my veins; I could actually see tributaries of gold, pink, and green light up underneath my skin. The herbs and roots around the graves began to writhe, twisting and spiraling as if alive, pushing through the ground with a ferocious urgency. Leaves unfurled in seconds, stems thickening and blooming at an unnatural speed. The ancient oaks groaned as their roots stirred beneath the earth, intertwining with the growing plants. A variety of scents warred for supremacy—woody, floral, spicy, sweet—with the earthy smell of humus underneath. I spun around, laughing like a madwoman as a veritable Eden emerged in the cemetery. I ran from tree to tree, touching the bark and watching flowers bloom from nowhere under my fingertips. Everywhere I touched, flowers, herbs, and green plants sprang to life. The light in my blood faded but I could still feel the magic thrumming through me. Never in my life had it felt so strong, so present. I was nearly overwhelmed.

Verlean and Granma watched me, smiling wide. Mama stood a little apart, her lips pressed together in a tight line, her expression much more subdued.

“Thank you,” I told her.

She gave me a small nod of encouragement, her arms wrapped around herself.

Four generations rooted in the dirt, three on one side of eternity, one on the other. I gave them one last glance before heading back to my car. A ping on my phone alerted me to an email—the paperwork was done and ready to sign. I almost deleted Cutler’s message, but turning him down in person would be more satisfying.

Back at the farm, the fields bloomed for me as I walked through them, the herbs, plants, and roots doubling, tripling in size. It was yet night, but I lifted my gaze to the fields and farms beyond ours. My palms itched with power.

I had a lot to do.

Verdell Walker is a writer of speculative fiction from rural Georgia whose work is inspired by her heritage and her research. Her stories are in *Tractor Beam* and *Reckoning*, while her nonfiction writing has appeared in *Bustle*, *Vox*, *Forge*, and *ZORA*. She can be found on Instagram: @verdellwalkerwrites and Substack: @verdellwalker, as well as her book review podcast, The Book Up.

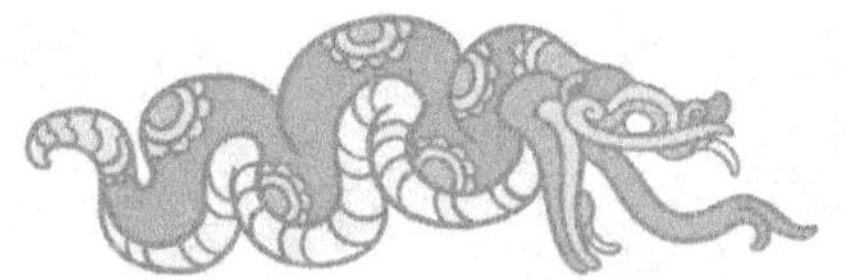

Daydreams and Wooden Shutters

Mike Wheeler

Michael Temi-tope Adebiyi (Mike Wheeler) is a fine-art photographer from Ilorin, Nigeria, whose expressionist, surrealist work explores identity and human experience. His photography has been featured in *Lolwe*, *Blue Marble Review*, *Josephine Quarterly*, *Chestnut Review*, *Spellbinder*, and *Ake Review*, with exhibitions in New York (Canvas Gallery), Bali (Superlative Gallery), Nairobi (ETH Safari), and Lisbon (NFC Summit).

The Power of the Land

Odega Shawa

1.

I remember the soil first. When I reached in and filled a farm trowel with it, damp, red, breathing under the greenery, it clung to my fingers like memory. It felt like something alive. It was alive, duh. But I mean something different. The soil felt like it was *intelligent*. Like it knew what was going on. Like it knew what was about to happen, the evil that was about to befall it. From we humans, of course.

In Abronoma, we didn't just walk on the land—we listened to it. The forest spoke in rustling leaves. Insects were part of nature's low hum. Crickets were the flutists of the forest knowledge orchestra. My father used to say the trees had tongues, and if you were quiet enough, they'd tell you secrets older than the city.

I was eighteen the day the forest whispered its final warning.

The morning began like any other. I woke to the sound of my mother grinding maize. The rhythm was steady and familiar. My younger siblings—Kweku and little Ama—chased each other around the compound. Their laughter bounced off the clay walls. My father was already in the grove, tending to the cocoa trees. I joined him after breakfast. I had one of our farm machetes in hand, ready to clear the underbrush and check for pests.

We worked in silence. We usually do. It was the kind of silence that only comes from years of shared labor. The sun filtered through the canopy in golden shafts. And the air smelled of damp earth and ripe fruit. I loved that smell. It was the scent of home, of history. Our farm wasn't just land—it was legacy. And it was lineage. My grandfather had planted the first trees here. My father added the yam beds. I had just begun carving out a corner for cassava. Already, I was dreaming of building a small hut there one day. Maybe with Abena, if she ever said yes.

But the forest was uneasy that morning.

Birds flew low and fast, their calls sharp and erratic. The wind carried a metallic tang, like rust and smoke. I paused, listening. There it was again—a low, grinding sound, unnatural, like metal chewing stone. My father looked up, his brow furrowed.

'You hear that, dad?' I asked.

He nodded slowly. 'That's not the forest.'

We followed the sound. With our machetes gripped tight in our hands, our hearts pounded. There had been rumors. But nothing had happened on our side so far. The disquiet in our hearts said it might be, it was our turn. The path led us past the yam beds, beyond the sacred grove where no one was allowed to cut trees. That was where we saw them—men in yellow boots, helmets, and vests. Machines roared behind them, tearing into the earth like hungry beasts. The trees fell like wounded animals, their trunks splintering, roots exposed and bleeding.

Galamsey.

I'd heard the word whispered in the village, always with fear, always with dread. Illegal gold miners. They came like cannibal ghosts, digging in secret, poisoning rivers, bribing chiefs. But this—this was no secret. It was an invasion.

My father stepped forward, shouting. 'This is sacred land! You have no right!'

One of the men turned, his face hidden behind a mask. He raised a rifle.

I grabbed my father's arm. 'Let's go. We need the elders.'

The man fired into the air, and the forest went silent.

We ran.

Back at the compound, my mother was already gathering the children. My sister Abena had returned from the stream, her face pale. 'They're everywhere,' she said. 'They've blocked the road.'

The elders came quickly, their staffs clutched like weapons. They tried to reason, to speak of land rights and ancestral covenants. But the men in yellow boots didn't care. They had papers—forged, no doubt—and guns. One of them laughed when Nana Kwame spoke of the spirits.

'Your gods can't stop progress,' the stranger said. 'Gold is gold.'

That night, we didn't sleep. We kept watch, machetes and bows in hand. The forest groaned under the weight of machines. Smoke rose in the distance. I held Ama close, whispering stories of the river god who protected children. She asked if the god would protect us. I said yes. I lied.

At dawn, they appeared in our compound. No warning. No mercy.

Shots rang out. My father fell first, clutching his chest. My mother screamed, shielding Ama. A bullet tore through her shoulder. Abena tried to run, but they caught her. Kweku—my brave little brother—threw a stone and was shot in the back.

I charged, machete raised, heart pounding. I didn't think. I didn't feel. I just moved.

I reached one of them, slashed his arm. He cried out. Another raised his gun. I saw the muzzle flash. Then—nothing. No pain. No sound. Just silence. It was like plunging into a deep pond from a formidable height. It was the same deafening silence. The same weightlessness.

And then I was floating.

Above the compound. Above the blood-soaked soil. My body lay twisted, eyes wide, mouth open. My mother crawled toward me, dragging Ama. Abena screamed. The forest burned.

I tried to speak. To shout. To move. But I was air. Smoke. Memory suspended in wind. I hovered above the ruins of my life, watching the men laugh, watching the trees fall, watching the river turn black.

The forest whispered again.

But this time, it spoke to me. But it wasn't words it spoke. It spoke images. In timeless sequence I saw words as images. Coming. Going. Tractors. Rifles. Shootings. Trees. Streams. Rivers. The ocean. Farms. Yam. Corn. Cocoa. Pests. Pets. Violence. Blood. Harmony. Disharmony. Cadence. Broken. Greed. Shame. Shameless. Cruel. Brutal.

It felt scorching to read images of communication not supposed to be carried with sounds. Then the sounds hit, with sensory overload. The words quickly reassembled themselves. It was like being dashed into ice-cold water. I started screaming. But even though I floated above them, the men that shot us continued laughing and smoking, almost as if I had stopped existing.

I woke up from the nightmare, screaming.

2.

I used to think evil wore a suit, that it came in the form of men with briefcases and polished shoes, speaking English too clean for the red soil of Abronoma. But I was wrong. Evil came to us in yellow boots.

They arrived three days after the first explosion. Not quietly. Not respectfully. Their trucks roared through the village like beasts, kicking up dust and drowning out the birdsong. The elders gathered at the square. Worry carved their faces with dread and powerlessness. I stood behind my father, machete in hand. My heart thudded like a drum.

The men wore helmets and reflective vests, their boots thick with mud. One of them—tall, pale-skinned, with a clipboard—stepped forward and smiled like he was selling soap. 'We're here to help,' he said. 'Your land is rich. We want to make you rich too.'

Nana Kwame, our oldest elder, stepped forward. His voice was calm, but firm. 'This land is not for sale. It is sacred. It feeds us. It buries our dead. And raises our children. We have nothing else but the land.'

The man laughed. 'We have permits. Signed by the government district office. We're backed by investors. You'll be compensated.'

Compensated. As if the river could be paid for. As if the trees could be bought. As if the forest could be replaced by the men in yellow boots. They never replaced anything. The rumors that arrived before them said so.

They offered bribes first. Bags of rice. Bottles of schnapps. Envelopes thick with cedis. Some of the younger men hesitated. Hunger makes the soul soft. But the elders refused. My father spat at their feet.

That night, the threats began.

Men in dark clothes walked the village paths, whispering. Chickens vanished. A hut burned. My friend Kojo found a bullet casing on his doorstep. Abena, my sister, woke to find a dead bird nailed to our door.

We knew what it meant. They weren't just here for gold. They were here to erase us, to displace us.

So we organized.

Kojo and I formed a group—just five of us at first, youths who knew the forest better than any map. We called ourselves 'Asase Tumi', The Power of Land. Abena joined too, her eyes fierce, her voice sharper than any blade. We met in secret, beneath the old baobab, where the spirits were said to listen. We planned sabotage. We mapped the mining paths. We tracked their trucks. We learned their routines.

But the land was already changing. The river turned cloudy. Frogs died. Fish floated belly-up. Children began coughing. Ama, my little sister, refused to drink. She said the water tasted like metal. Crops wilted. The yam beds turned yellow. The cocoa pods shriveled. My mother wept as she dug up a row of cassava—each root black and soft. The elders prayed. They poured libations. They sang to the spirits.

But the forest was restless, the prayers useless. I felt it in the wind. It no longer whispered—it hissed. The trees leaned away from the mining site, as if recoiling. Birds stopped nesting. Even the ants moved their colonies.

One night, I dreamt of fire. The grove was burning. My ancestors stood in the flames, silent. When I woke, my hands smelled of smoke.

Kojo said he had the same dream.

We knew we had to act.

That evening, under the cover of darkness, Kojo and I crept toward the mining camp. We wore black, smeared our faces with charcoal. The machines were silent now, sleeping like monsters. Guards patrolled lazily, their rifles slung low.

We slipped past them, hearts pounding. The camp was a maze of tents and metal containers. We found one labeled 'Operations'. Inside, maps and documents littered a table. Kojo held the flashlight while I scanned the papers.

That's when I saw it: a map. Detailed. Precise. At the top, in bold red letters: 'Abronoma: Extraction Zone.' Our village. Our farms. Our sacred grove. All marked for destruction.

I felt something break inside me.

Kojo swore under his breath. 'They're planning to take everything.'

I nodded, my fists clenched. 'We need to show the elders.'

But before we could move, we heard footsteps. Heavy. Fast.

We ducked behind crates as two men entered. One of them was the pale-skinned man from before. The other wore a suit—clean, pressed, out of place. They spoke in low tones.

'The villagers are resisting,' the suited man said. 'We may need to escalate.'

The pale man shrugged. 'We have the permits. The police are on our side. If they push, we push harder.'

'And the spirits?'

The pale man laughed. 'Superstition. Trees don't fight back.'

I wanted to scream. To leap out and show him how wrong he was. But Kojo grabbed my arm.

We waited until they left. Then we took the map and fled.

As we ran through the forest, the wind howled. The trees shook. I swear I heard a voice—low, ancient, angry. Abronoma is bleeding. But it was just my inner fear escalating through my thoughts. I am hearing my own fear.

We reached the village breathless, the map clutched in my hand. The elders gathered. We showed them everything.

Nana Kwame's face darkened. 'They mean to erase us.'

My father nodded. 'Then we must become become difficult to erase.'

That night, the forest didn't sleep. And neither did I.

But we saw flashlights tear at the sky over us. It was from the new work site of the invaders. I remember the plan I stole. The contents said it was done for Groupa Company Ltd. I knew Groupa. It was a drilling and mining company owned by a group of powerful capitalists operating out of Accra. Even as I was thinking this, a helicopter roared into earshot. I ran outside, as did my father and mother. Lights bleeped and beeped from the monstrous mosquito. It was headed to the new mine site.

3.

I used to think my grandmother's stories were just that—stories. She'd sit under the moonlight, her voice low and thick like palm wine, telling us about the spirits that lived in the silk-cotton trees and the river gods who punished greed. I'd listen, half-believing, half-dreaming. But after the map, after the whispers in the wind, I stopped doubting.

The forest was speaking.

It began with the trees. They creaked at night, even when the air was still. Leaves rustled without wind. I'd walk past the grove and feel watched—not by animals, but by something older. Something buried deep in the roots.

One morning, I heard a voice. Not loud. Not human.

It came from the baobab. 'They dig. We bleed.'

I froze. Kojo was beside me, sharpening a blade. I turned to him. 'Did you hear that?'

He looked up, confused. 'Hear what?'

I didn't answer. I just stared at the tree, its bark pulsing like a heartbeat.

We had no time to dwell on ghosts. The resistance was growing. Nsuo Tumi had swelled to twelve members—young, angry, determined. We met every night, planning sabotage, mapping escape routes, gathering tools. Abena had drawn up a list of targets: fuel tanks, generators, water pumps. We didn't want blood. We wanted disruption.

'If we hit their machines,' she said, 'we hit their money.'

Kojo nodded. 'And if we hit their money, they'll feel us.'

Our first strike was simple. We poured sugar into the fuel tanks of two bulldozers. By morning, they were coughing black smoke and grinding to a halt. The miners cursed and kicked the machines. We watched from the trees, silent and satisfied.

The second strike was bolder. We cut the cables to their water pumps, the ones draining the river to wash gold. That night, the frogs returned. The river sang again.

But they retaliated. They brought more guards. More guns. They patrolled the village, flashing permits and sneering. One of them spat at Nana Kwame's feet. 'This land belongs to the state now,' he said. 'You people are just squatting.'

The elders called for a protest. It was peaceful, at first. We marched to the edge of the mining site, holding signs made from old cassava sacks. We sang songs of the land, of ancestors, of justice. My father led the chants, his voice strong despite the years. 'Abronoma is not for sale!'

But they didn't care.

Police arrived in trucks, faces hidden behind masks. They fired tear gas without warning. The air turned white. People screamed. Children ran. I saw Abena fall, clutching her eyes. Kojo dragged her away.

My father stood his ground. A baton cracked against his ribs.I ran to him, coughing, blind. I grabbed his arm, pulled him back. He collapsed beside me, gasping.

'They beat me,' he whispered. 'They beat the land.'

We hid in the grove that night, nursing wounds and rage. The forest wrapped around us like a blanket. The air was thick with fog—unnatural, dense, glowing faintly. It moved like it had purpose. Kojo stared at it. 'Where did this come from?'

I didn't answer. I just listened.

'Protect. Resist. Remember.'

The voice again. Clearer now. It came from everywhere—the trees, the soil, the wind. I looked up. The branches swayed, though the air was still. 'The forest is helping us,' I said.

Kojo frowned. 'You sound like your grandmother.'

I smiled. 'Maybe she was right.'

We used the fog to strike again. It covered our movements, muffled our steps. We snuck into the camp, slashed tires, stole documents. The guards couldn't see us, couldn't hear us. It was like the land wanted revenge.

But revenge has a price.

The next day, I returned home to find smoke rising from our farm. The yam beds were ash. The cocoa trees were black skeletons.

Our farm hut was gone.

I dropped to my knees. A bullet casing lay in the soil. I picked it up. It was warm.

That was when I knew. They weren't just mining gold. They planned to exterminate us. We had tried to warn the elders. But it was useless. We had to do something ourselves.

That night we went out to the mining site again. We moved in silence, crouched low beneath the ridge, the mine site glowing like a wound in the earth. Kojo checked his watch—2:17 a.m. The guards were rotating. Abena handed me the wire cutters. Our target was the generator powering the water pumps. 'Quick in, quick out,' she whispered. 'No more, no less.'

We split into pairs. I followed Kojo through the shadows, heart thudding. The air reeked of diesel and river rot. We reached the fence, clipped it clean, and slipped through. The generator hummed like a sleeping beast.

Kojo knelt, pulled out the sugar packets. I kept watch.

Then—crack. A gunshot split the night.

'Run!' someone shouted.

Lights flared. Alarms screamed. I saw Mensah drop, clutching his chest. Blood soaked his shirt. He didn't move. Abena screamed. Kojo grabbed her arm and dragged her toward the fence. I turned to help Mensah, but another shot rang out. Something hot tore through my shoulder. I hit the ground hard.

'Addo!' Kojo was back, pulling me up. I staggered, pain blinding. We ran, bullets slicing the air. The fence loomed ahead—Kojo shoved me through, then Abena.

Mensah was still inside.

We couldn't go back. We sprinted into the bush, branches slashing our faces, lungs burning. Behind us, the mine roared to life, guards shouting, dogs barking.

We collapsed near the river, bleeding, broken. Kojo didn't speak. Abena sobbed quietly.

Mensah was gone.

When day broke, we found his body on the road leading to the Accra Highway. We carried it back to the village to give it a proper burial. The elders remonstrated with us. But we were past caring now. It was war—and we were not the ones who declared it.

4.

I knew they would come. After Mensah's death, after the sabotage, after the sugar in their fuel tanks and the cables we sliced clean, there was no question. The mine site had become a fortress overnight. More guards. More guns. Fewer questions. We had struck a nerve.

But I didn't expect them to come for my family.

It started with the dogs. I heard them barking just after midnight—low, guttural, not the usual village strays. These were trained, angry, and close. I sat up in the hut, heart pounding. My father was already awake, machete in hand. My mother clutched Ama to her chest. Abena peeked through the window. 'They're here,' she whispered.

Outside, the moon lit up the compound in pale silver. Shadows moved between the trees. Boots crunched on dry leaves. I counted at least six men—rifles slung, flashlights sweeping.

Kojo had warned me earlier that day: 'They're not just protecting the mine anymore. They're hunting.' I didn't want to believe him.

My father stepped outside first, hands raised. 'This is our home,' he said. 'We are not criminals.'

A flashlight blinded him. A voice barked orders. 'Down! On the ground!'

I stepped out behind him, fists clenched. Abena followed, her voice steady. 'We haven't done anything wrong.'

The man in front—tall, broad-shouldered, face hidden behind a mask—raised his rifle. 'You sabotaged government property. You're harboring fugitives. You're done.'

My father didn't move. 'This land is ours. You have no right.'

The man fired. The sound split the night. My father staggered, clutching his side. Blood soaked his shirt. My mother screamed. Ama cried out. I lunged forward, catching him before he hit the ground.

'Baba!' I shouted.

Another shot rang out—this time toward the hut. The wall splintered. Abena pulled Ama back inside.

I dragged my father behind the water drum, pressing cloth to his wound. He was breathing, barely. 'Stay with me,' I whispered.

Outside, chaos erupted. More gunfire. Screams. I saw Nana Kwame fall near the grove, his staff broken beside him. Two other elders collapsed in the dust. The guards moved like a swarm, kicking down doors, dragging people out.

The forest didn't make a sound. No birds. No wind. No insects. Just silence.

I ran toward the back of the compound, hoping to flank them, maybe draw them away. I didn't think. I just moved. A guard spotted me, raised his weapon. I ducked behind the cassava shed, grabbed a rusted hoe, and hurled it. It missed. He fired. The bullet grazed my leg. I fell hard, rolled, and crawled toward the bush.

Behind me, I heard Abena shouting. Then a crack. Then nothing. I reached the edge of the grove and collapsed.

The next morning, the village was ash. The elders were dead. My father was unconscious. My mother had fled with Ama. Abena was missing. The compound was burned. The yam beds were gone. The cocoa trees were black stumps.I walked through the ruins, limping, dazed. The air smelled of smoke and blood. Chickens pecked at the dirt, confused. A dog whined near the stream.

Other farmers had fled. The ones who stayed moved like ghosts.

Kojo found me near the broken drum. 'They killed Nana,' he said. 'And Elder Badu. And Elder Serwaa.'

I nodded. I couldn't speak.

'Your sister?'

'I don't know.'

He sat beside me, silent. We didn't cry. We didn't scream. We just stared.

That night, I couldn't sleep. My leg throbbed. My hands shook. I kept replaying the moment—my father falling, the gunfire, the silence. I lay on the floor of Kojo's hut, staring at the ceiling.

And then I dreamed.

I was back in the compound, but everything was frozen. The trees were still. The air was thick. The sky was gray. I walked through the ruins, barefoot, bleeding.

A figure stood near the grove, not glowing, not floating, just standing, old, tall, wrapped in cloth, face hidden in shadow. He didn't speak at first. Then he turned to me. 'You are not done.'

I woke with a jolt, drenched in sweat.

Kojo stirred beside me. 'You okay?'

I nodded. 'Just a dream.' But it didn't feel like one. It felt like a warning.

The next morning, I limped to the stream. The water was low, cloudy. Frogs were gone. The trees leaned away from the bank, as if ashamed. I washed my face, stared at my reflection. I didn't recognize myself. My cheek was bruised. My eyes were hollow. My hands trembled.

I thought of my father, still unconscious. My mother, somewhere in the hills. Abena, missing. I thought of Nana Kwame, lying in the dust. And I thought of the man in the mask. I clenched my fists.

We had tried peace. We had tried protest. We had tried sabotage. They answered with bullets.

I walked back to the village square. Kojo was there, speaking to the remaining youths. Some were wounded. Some were angry. All were afraid.

'They want us gone,' he said. 'They want the land. The gold. The silence.'

I stepped forward. 'Then we give them noise.'

They turned to me.

'We regroup. We rebuild. We fight smarter. No more direct attacks. No more open protests. We hit their supply lines. We expose their lies. We document everything.'

Kojo nodded. 'We go public.'

Abena had once mentioned a journalist in Accra—someone who covered land rights and mining corruption. I remembered her name. I wrote it down. We would send photos. Names. Maps. Testimonies. We would make Abronoma visible.

That night, we buried the elders. No drums. No songs. Just silence. And resolve.

5.

The morning after the burial, the village was quiet. Not peaceful—just hollow. The kind of silence that comes after something has been taken and nothing has replaced it. The elders were gone. The farms were scorched. The river was poisoned. And the people of Abronoma were tired. But not broken.

Kojo and I sat under the charred remains of the baobab tree, the one where we used to meet with Nsuo Tumi. He was sharpening a blade, not for farming, but for defense. I was scribbling names on a torn piece of cardboard—names of villagers who had witnessed the attacks, who had lost someone, who had something to say.

'We need to document everything,' I said. 'Photos. Testimonies.

Dates. Names. If we can't fight them with weapons, we fight them with truth.'

Kojo nodded. 'And we need to get it out. Beyond Abronoma. To Accra. To the world.'

We remembered the journalist Abena had mentioned before she disappeared—Efua Mensimah, known for exposing corrupt land deals and illegal mining operations. Kojo had a cousin in the city who owed him a favor. We decided to send a package: a flash drive with photos of the destruction, a handwritten letter, and a copy of the map we'd stolen from the mine site.

That afternoon, we gathered what we could. I borrowed Kojo's old phone, cracked but still working. We walked through the village, taking pictures—burned huts, poisoned crops, the graves of the elders. We interviewed survivors. My mother, still shaken, spoke softly about the night they fled. A farmer named Yaw showed us the bullet holes in his water tank. A young girl, no older than ten, described the taste of the river water: 'It burns my throat.' We compiled everything.

Kojo's cousin came at night, on a motorbike, wearing a hoodie and carrying a backpack. He didn't stay long. Just took the package, nodded once, and sped off into the dark.

'If she's real,' Kojo said, 'she'll know what to do.'

But we couldn't wait for help.The mine was expanding. We saw new trucks arrive, loaded with equipment. The guards were more aggressive, patrolling the village perimeter, stopping people at random. They built a new fence—taller, barbed, with floodlights that lit up the forest like a prison yard.

We needed eyes inside.

That's when we found Kwabena. He was seventeen, quiet, and worked as a cook's assistant at the mine site. His uncle had forced him into the job, saying it was better than starving. But Kwabena hated them. He'd seen too much—guards beating workers, chemicals dumped into the river, bribes exchanged in plain sight. 'I'll help,' he said. 'But if they catch me, I'm dead.'

We gave him a burner phone and instructions. Every night, he sent us updates—photos of documents, audio recordings of conversations, even a video of a guard threatening a farmer.

One night, he sent a message that changed everything. "They're planning a full-scale expansion. They want to clear the rest of the grove by next week. They're bringing in explosives."

Explosives. That meant they weren't just mining anymore.

They were erasing.

We called an emergency meeting. Only fifteen people showed up. The rest were either too scared or had fled. We laid out the plan: a blockade. We'd gather at the grove entrance, chain ourselves to the trees, and refuse to move. Peaceful. Visible. Defiant.

'They'll bring the police,' someone said.

'Let them,' I replied. 'We'll have cameras. We'll have witnesses. If they attack us again, the world will see.'

We spent the next two days preparing. We made signs from old roofing sheets. We printed photos and taped them to sticks. We rehearsed chants. Kojo taught the younger ones how to link arms and hold formation.

The night before the blockade, I couldn't sleep. I walked to the grove alone, flashlight in hand. The trees stood tall, silent. I touched one, its bark rough against my palm. I thought of my father, still recovering. My sister, still missing. The elders, buried beneath the soil. I whispered, not to spirits, but to myself. 'We won't let them win.'

The next morning, we gathered at dawn. Twenty-seven villagers. Some old, some young. All determined. We stood at the grove entrance, signs raised, voices loud.

'Abronoma is not for sale!'

'Protect our land!'

'No more blood for gold!'

The guards arrived first, confused, unsure. Then the police—four trucks, riot gear, tear gas. They formed a line, shields up, batons ready. A man in a suit stepped forward. I recognized him from the mine site—the operations manager. 'You are trespassing on government property,' he said. 'Disperse immediately.'

I stepped forward. 'This is our land. Our farms. Our homes. You are the trespassers.'

He didn't respond. Just nodded to the police. They moved fast.

Tear gas canisters flew through the air. Smoke filled our lungs. People screamed. I held my ground, coughing, eyes burning. Kojo grabbed my arm. We fell back, regrouped behind the trees. Then the batons came.They beat us, dragged us, arrested five people. One woman collapsed. A boy was knocked unconscious.

But we didn't run. We filmed everything. Kojo's phone caught the entire assault: the signs, the chants, the violence.

That night, we uploaded the footage. We sent it to Efua Mensimah. We sent it to every journalist we could find. We sent it to the world.

And the world responded. Within forty eight hours, the video went viral. Thousands of views. Comments. Shares. People were outraged. Activists reached out. Lawyers offered help. A local radio station invited Kojo to speak.

But the mine didn't back down. They doubled security. They issued a statement calling us 'agitators' and 'saboteurs.' They claimed we were endangering national development.

Then they sent a warning, a note, slipped under Kojo's door. "You're next."

We didn't flinch. We planned another blockade. But this time, they didn't wait.

The night before the protest, I was walking back from the stream when I heard footsteps, fast, heavy. I turned. Two men in black rushed me.

I ran. Through the bush, over the ridge, toward the village. They chased me, shouting.

I tripped, hit the ground hard. One grabbed my shirt. I kicked, scrambled, broke free.

I reached Kojo's hut, slammed the door behind me. He looked up, startled. 'They tried to grab me,' I gasped.

He didn't speak, just handed me a machete.

6.

I didn't sleep after the attack. Every sound outside Kojo's hut felt like a footstep. Every shadow looked like a man with a gun. I kept the machete beside me, blade dull but comforting. Kojo slept with one eye open, twitching at every creak of the wooden walls.

We were being hunted.

The next morning, we gathered what was left of the resistance. Only nine of us now. The rest had either fled or gone silent. Some were afraid. Some were grieving. Some were just tired.

Kojo stood in front of the group, arms crossed, voice low. 'They're trying to break us. One by one. Door by door.'

'Then we hit back,' I said. 'Not with machetes. With exposure.'

We had one advantage left: the footage from the last protest had gone viral. Efua Mensimah had published a scathing article, naming the mining company, the district officials, and the police. She quoted villagers, showed photos of the destruction, even included a map of the planned expansion. It was everywhere.

But the mine didn't flinch. Instead, they accelerated. By midday, bulldozers were clearing the last stretch of forest near the river. The grove was gone. The trees were gone. The birds were gone.

And then the real shock came. Kojo's cousin, the one who had delivered our package to Efua, was found dead. His body was discovered in a ditch outside the next town. No ID. No phone. Just a broken wristwatch and a cracked helmet.

We got the news from a trader passing through. 'They said it was a robbery,' she told us. 'But no one believes that.'

Kojo didn't speak for hours. When he finally did, his voice was hollow. 'They're killing anyone who talks.'

I felt something shift inside me. Not fear, not grief. Resolve.

We couldn't wait for justice. We had to force it.

That night, we planned our most daring move yet. A full infiltration.

Kwabena, our contact inside the mine, had sent a message: the company was holding a private meeting with government officials at the site. No press, no oversight, just deals and signatures. "They're finalizing the expansion," he wrote. "Once it's signed, it's over."

We had one chance. Kojo, Abena—who had returned quietly two days earlier, bruised but alive—and I would sneak into the site during the meeting. We'd record everything. Names. Faces. Documents. We'd get proof of corruption, of collusion, of violence.

And we'd leak it.

We spent the next day preparing. Black clothes. Burner phones. A stolen ID badge from Kwabena. A route through the bush, mapped by memory and desperation.

We moved at dusk.

The mine site was lit like a stadium. Guards patrolled the perimeter, rifles slung, eyes scanning. Trucks rumbled. Generators hummed. The air smelled of oil and fear.

We crawled through the underbrush, hearts pounding. Kojo led, I followed, Abena covered the rear. We reached the fence, clipped it silently, and slipped through.

Inside, the camp was a maze of tents and containers. Kwabena had marked the meeting tent with a red cloth. We spotted it near the center, guarded by two men.

'We need a distraction,' Abena whispered.

Kojo nodded. 'Give me five minutes.' He vanished into the shadows.

Abena and I waited, crouched behind a stack of crates. My hands shook. My leg still ached from the bullet wound. I thought of my father, still recovering. My mother, still hiding. Kojo's cousin, lying in a ditch.

Then—bang. A loud crash echoed from the far end of the camp. Guards shouted. Lights swung. The two men at the tent ran toward the noise.

Kojo returned, breathless. 'I knocked over a fuel drum. They think it's sabotage.'

We slipped into the tent.

Inside, five men sat around a table. One wore a district uniform. Another had a company badge. The rest were in suits. Papers were spread out. A laptop glowed. We hid behind a stack of boxes and began recording.

'Once the expansion is approved,' one man said, 'we'll clear the rest of the valley. The villagers will be relocated.'

'What about the protests?' another asked.

'Handled. We've got the police on payroll. Anyone who resists disappears.'

Abena's hand tightened around the phone.

'And the journalist?'

'We're tracking her. She won't be a problem.'

Kojo's eyes widened.

We had enough. We slipped out, retraced our steps, and fled into the bush. By dawn, the footage was uploaded.

Efua called us directly. 'This is explosive,' she said. 'I'm sending it to every outlet I know.'

We thought we'd won. But we were wrong.

That afternoon, the mine site exploded. Not metaphorically. Literally.

A blast shook the valley, sending smoke and debris into the sky. The ground trembled. Trees fell. The river surged. We ran toward the site, fearing the worst.

What we found was chaos. The meeting tent was gone. The containers were twisted metal. Guards screamed. One man lay on the ground, bleeding from his ears.

And then we saw Kwabena. He was slumped against a truck, eyes wide, chest still. Dead.

I dropped to my knees. Kojo stared, silent. Abena turned away.

We didn't know what had happened. Sabotage? Accident? Retaliation?

But we knew one thing: they would blame us.

7.

We buried Kwabena in silence, no drums, no songs, just a shallow grave near the river, where the water still ran cloudy. His mother wept quietly, her hands trembling as she placed a stone on the mound. Kojo stood beside me, fists clenched, eyes hollow. 'They're not stopping,' he said. 'They're escalating.'

I nodded. 'Then so do we.'

The explosion at the mine site had rattled the valley, but it hadn't stopped the company. If anything, it made them more aggressive. They blamed us publicly, called us terrorists, accused us of sabotage. The district office issued a statement declaring Abronoma a "security risk zone." Police patrols doubled. Drones buzzed overhead. The grove was gone. The river was dying. And the people were being erased.

But the footage we leaked had done something. It had sparked a fire.

Journalists arrived. Activists reached out. Lawyers offered support. A human rights organization sent observers. Efua Mensimah published a second exposé, naming names, showing faces, quoting documents. The world was watching now. And the company knew it.

We intercepted a memo from inside the mine—Kwabena's last gift. It outlined their final plan: a full-scale clearing of the remaining farmland, followed by forced relocation of the villagers. They had approval from the district. They had security. They had a deadline. Three days.

We had three days to stop them.

We called a village assembly. Not in the square—too exposed—but in the old school building, half-collapsed but still standing. Everyone came. Farmers. Mothers. Youths. Even the elders who had survived the last raid.

Kojo stood at the front, voice steady. 'They want to finish us. We either fight now, or we lose everything.'

I stepped forward. 'This isn't just about Abronoma. It's about every village like ours. Every river poisoned. Every tree cut. Every voice silenced.'

We laid out the plan. A coordinated blockade. Not just at the mine site, but at the access roads, the fuel depot, the district office. We would divide into teams. Some would hold the line at the grove. Others would intercept supply trucks. A third group would march to the district office with petitions, photos, and testimonies. And we would livestream everything.

We had phones. We had networks. We had eyes.

'If they attack us,' Kojo said, 'the world will see.'

The villagers agreed.

We spent the next two days preparing. We built barricades from logs and scrap metal. We printed signs. We rehearsed chants. We trained the younger ones in nonviolent resistance—how to lock arms, how to stay grounded, how to protect each other.

The company prepared too. We saw new trucks arrive—armored, tinted. More guards. More weapons. Rumors spread of mercenaries hired from outside. The district office issued a curfew. Police checkpoints sprang up overnight. The air felt heavy, like something was about to break.

On the morning of the third day, we took our positions.

I stood at the grove entrance, machete sheathed, sign in hand: "This Land Is Our Life." Kojo led the road blockade, twenty villagers strong, dragging logs across the path and chaining themselves together. Abena marched toward the district office with a group of women, carrying petitions and photos.

The company moved fast. Trucks rolled in, engines snarling. Guards stepped out, rifles raised. A man in a suit shouted through a megaphone. 'Disperse immediately. This is a restricted zone.'

We didn't move. Kojo shouted back. 'This is our home. You are the trespassers.'

The guards advanced.

We locked arms.

The first clash came at the roadblock. Police fired tear gas. People screamed. Kojo held the line, coughing, eyes red. A woman collapsed. A boy was dragged away. But the cameras were rolling. The livestream showed everything.

At the grove, the guards tried to push through. I stood my ground.

One of them raised a baton. I braced for impact. Then—shouts.

Journalists arrived, cameras flashing. Observers from the human rights group stepped in, demanding restraint. The guards hesitated.

At the district office, Abena's group was denied entry. They sat on the steps, chanting, holding signs. Police tried to remove them. They resisted peacefully. The footage went viral.

By midday, the mine was paralyzed. Trucks couldn't move. Roads were blocked. The district office was flooded with calls. The company issued a statement denying wrongdoing. But the damage was done.

And then the final shock came. A whistleblower from inside the district office leaked documents—signed approvals, bribe records, emails between officials and the company.

It was all there: corruption, collusion, cover-ups. Efua published it within hours.

The government responded. An emergency investigation was launched. The mine's operations were suspended. The district commissioner was arrested. The company's license was revoked. We had won. Not with machetes. With truth.

The next morning, the trucks left. The guards disappeared. The machines went silent. And the forest, what was left of it, breathed again.

We stood in the grove, Kojo beside me, Abena holding Ama's hand. My father, still weak, smiled for the first time in weeks. The villagers gathered, not to protest, but to plant. Yams. Cassava. Cocoa. The land was scarred, but alive.

And we were still here.

Six months after the final confrontation, Abronoma is no longer a forgotten dot on a corrupted map. The mine is gone. The machines were dismantled, the guards withdrawn. The district commissioner was tried and sentenced. The company's license was revoked, and its name became a cautionary tale in every newsroom from Accra to Abuja.

The villagers rebuilt slowly. The land, though scarred, began to heal. Yams sprouted again. The river, once poisoned, ran clearer each week. Children returned to school. The grove, though reduced, was replanted with saplings—each one named after someone we lost.

Kojo now leads a regional coalition against illegal mining. Abena teaches environmental law in the city, returning every month to walk the paths she once defended. My father recovered, though he walks with a limp. My mother still hums when she cooks, her voice softer but steady. And me? I remain a name carved into a stone near the grove. A story told at dusk.

Odega Shawa is a Lagos, Nigeria based freelance writer and poet with two published novels and a couple of non-fiction books. He has battled Major Depressive Disorder and schizophrenia all his life and has just managed to attain a First Class Honors from the National Open University of Nigeria, having graduated with a B.Sc in Peace Studies and Conflict Resolution. Writing, to Odega, is both hobby and escape. His deepest motive is to use his writing to create a better world for every living thing on earth.

He has also edited a poetry anthology: *84 Delicious Bottles of Red Wine for Wole Soyinka*. The special edition publication is in honor of Africa's first Nobel Prize in Literature winner, Professor Wole Soyinka's 84th birthday festivities and the anthology was personally endorsed by the Nobel laureate.

Recollection

Adegboyega Kayowa

During my grandmother's prayers, I would watch
the cracked earth just outside her windowpane, the dust lifting

like sermons lost in the dry air. My favorite story
was of the river that once carved through the valley,

its body endless, spilling into the fields. Less famous
is how the Big Pharm diverted it, how the heat pressed

its lips against the banks until nothing remained
but brittle bones of fish in the silt. And when the sky opened

and rain poured over us, my grandmother knelt,
cupped her hands, and drank. I wonder if she felt

the phantom taste of the old river on her tongue,
if she saw its face in the ripples, its body returning

only to disappear again. This is what I thought about
until her prayers ended, when she took my hand,

waiting for the soil to soften beneath us,
as birds pecked at the hardened ground.

Adegboyega Kayowa is a writer and teacher whose work has appeared in *Analog Science Fiction and Fact* Magazine, *Queen's Quarterly*, *Bi+ Lines* Anthology and other publications. In addition to her writing, she works as a copy editor. She lives with two German Shepherds and two neurotic cats.

Burn Barrel Astrology

Fendy S. Tulodo

My uncle swears you can tell what kind of man someone is
by how he stacks wood in a burn barrel.
We don't use those anymore but he still talks like they matter.
Still keeps one in the back, rusted and dented, filled with junk mail and busted dreams.
The landfill's too far now,
gas is too high,
and they shut down bus service out here.
So we've been stuffing old campaign signs into our fireplace.
Most of them say something about "freedom."
I can't help laughing when the letters curl.
He said the stars used to line up different
back before the big box stores came.
Back before they paved over the wetland.
Now nothing aligns right.
Even the deer are confused.
They built condos where the beavers lived.
Then named them "Beaver Creek Estates."
My cousin spit on the sign when he drove by.
Said he saw one of the beavers limping down the shoulder,
dragging a piece of its home in its mouth.
Uncle says: next time,
we burn the maps.
We stop pretending this was ever about directions.
We follow the birds instead.
If they leave, we leave.
But I don't think they're leaving.
I saw two finches building a nest
in the side mirror of my neighbor's busted car.
That's got to mean something.
Right?

Fendy writes from Malang, Indonesia. He works in the motorcycle industry and finds poems in forgotten objects, roadside birds, and the silence between questions. His writing often follows what is overlooked and refuses to be mapped.

Botany of the Mouth

Rowan Tate

Rowan Tate is a Romanian creative and curator of beauty. Her writing appears in *The Stinging Fly*, *The Shore*, *Josephine Quarterly*, and *Meniscus Literary Journal*, among others. She reads nonfiction nature books, the backs of shampoo bottles, and sometimes minds.

On Leafing

Dyani Sabin

2020

It is March.
I have slept through my alarm every day this week.
Confusion until the silence of dawn reveals
that commuters are no longer driving past my windowsill
where a dahlia tuber, freshly buried in dirt, prepares for spring.
Their bodies roused my body
and so we met the day together.
No more.

It is April.
Furnace on, wearing shorts in my apartment. The next day turns—
burrowed in blankets. A paper wreath "happy birthday," hand-made crown,
delivered to the desolate planter outside my door. Celebrate on zoom.
A leaf appears in potted soil.
To welcome the dahlia, I call my grandmother.
Put it outside after the first full moon in June,
she says.

It is May.
Masked, I walk the dog past a battle for the soul
of a neighboring building, narrated for grandma on the phone.
Delicate floral arrangements cover one side,
the other arrayed in plastic leis, a mask made of a Walgreens bag, and a painting of shoes.
Already the city swelters, I move the dahlias outside, early.
In Maine, the snowdrops and crocuses have appeared, like jewels
to match grandma's pearls and the nineteen
dahlias that cohabitate on her bedroom windowsill.

It is June.
Gunshots.
Full moon rising, marchers wear black, kettled in the streets,
heat sinking into our bones even at night, trapped concrete to concrete.
At eighty-eight, grandma works to help Somali immigrants
establish roots in Maine, her hands steady as she embeds dahlias in the soil.

My plant is joined by signs for black lives
as we sit on my window ledge, together. Ten full inches of the outdoors.
My grandmother delights over my first bloom,
as I read Jane Austen to her and wave at masked walkers.

It is July.
Grandma reports on her evening news
viewing, grief spoken between the flowers of our gardens.
Too hot to sleep, midnight, I walk to the lake, check
for cops, the algae bloom report, sneak onto the beach where
neighbors sit in the inky surf. Crawl into the waves. Float. We hold our
breath as headlights pass. In the day, only the ticket attendant claims
the sand. Rip tides worry grandma, so these ablutions remain secret.
Mandolin strings against my fingers, I play for her
the words of the song sticky in my throat.
She claps, and tells me it was her father's favorite instrument.
Her dahlias have finally opened.

It is August.
I should be
in her garden, kitchen, surrounded by her dahlias, now
I sit with only my single plant, grandma on zoom. I walk in the cemetery,
make friends with the geese and the crows, coyotes,
squirrels, the American kestrel. My sketchbook fills with tombs.
I trace the lines of every Mary statue, angel, and Jesus of stone.
The lake is no match for the ice of the Atlantic, the numb joy of it,
but there are sharks this year—we are all in the wrong bodies of water.
Still, she tells me of music, of Poledark, the quiet press
of summer.

September.
My grandmother has a stroke.
I close my eyes as I pass the grave with her maiden name
carved across its front.

October.
She holds on.
"I'll vote for Joe Biden and Sara Gideon if it's the last thing I do."
Her largest smile, crooked,
while she signs her ballot. Heat wave, I swim again, think of her
stroke so steady next to mine. Lake turns to salt water.

I write to everyone I know, and many I don't of this
smile. Of duty and how she said "this election is unlike anything
I have lived through." And
she lives to vote, but does not see the election.
She'd tell me to cut my dahlia and store it for the winter but instead
it fades out on my balcony, a final fall of grace.

It is November.
First the freeze. Breath held. Thaw.
Masked chorus of honks and cheers. In the street my
neighbor sets off fireworks in the warm sun. Another
marches accompanied only by her tambourine. With nothing
but my voice, a smile, I join. We spin like the dry oak leaves,
rattle in the wind. Never-ending summer, a turning.
Months-late while aerating lawns, or on porches in t-shirts, others
sing. Like summertime, like beaches, park cookouts, the fourth of July,
as if we were shoulder-to-shoulder, what used to count as city solitude.
Alone, I walk home along an alley and among
the dead, dry weeds between the asphalt and the cemetery fence
a dahlia still blooms.

Dyani Sabin is a queer author of speculative fiction, poetry, and science journalism. Her work has been published in *Strange Horizons, Enchanted Conversations, Reckoning, Vastarien, Vast Chasm, Small Wonders,* as well as *National Geographic, The Washington Post*, and *Popular Science*. You can find her haunting a cornfield, @dyanisabin.bsky.social or at dyanisabin.com.

Reclamation

J. L. Rifkin

"Your shuttle will arrive in—four!—minutes. Please proceed to—Caladan Avenue."

Benny tapped the air above the "Dismiss notification" button on her HUD. She'd been at the shuttle stop for twelve minutes already, and wished she'd taken the time to pee before she left.

Her leg, both where it was and where it wasn't, felt weird.

She flipped through her notifications. "Reminder—two!—overdue assignments in Reentry Journal. You can do it! To access writing coach, press—"

She dismissed it and loaded the block puzzle game.

The shuttle chimed an arpeggio when it stopped. The lift extended automatically when it detected her ID. She held the handrest—"Please hold handrest securely! Lifting!"—and slipped into the first empty pod.

She was actually supposed to be practicing with stairs. Maybe the shuttle software didn't get the memo.

She tabbed back to the block game.

Benny waited until everyone else was off to leave her pod. She didn't want people watching while the lift beeped its excruciating way down.

Outside, a blue and white sign read "Puente Hills Reclamation Facility: Treasure For Tomorrow." Around the sign, her HUD displayed a wheel of floating menu buttons: "Book a Tour," "Careers," "Materials Reclaimed," "For Kids!"

Graeme was waiting at the gates, a sturdy block of a woman with gray in her ponytail.

"Benny! You made it! Welcome. We'll do HR first and then I'll give you the tour. Sound good?"

Benny's new access badge looked just like Graeme's. Kinda nice, Benny thought. Retro.

"Okay! Next stop, locker room. There's bathrooms there too, if you need them. We shower in, we shower out. Inside, you wear scrubs. No outside clothes in the containment zone, no scrubs outside the containment zone. Got it?" She waited for Benny's nod before continuing, "Anything metal, you can keep on. There'll be scrubs and booties when you come out. Everything fits weird. Oh, and put your leg through on the tool cycle—that's what I do with my hand."

Graeme waved her right hand, and Benny finally noticed that it was printed plastic, its phalanges and metacarpals articulated in black, silver, and hot pink.

Her new leg was gray. That was the default when you didn't enter color choices.

Graeme kept smiling until Benny closed the shower cubicle door behind her. It was a narrow room with labeled panels on the wall. Too narrow—she couldn't stretch her arms—couldn't move—her pulse sped up—she couldn't move! Shit! No—come on—she closed her eyes and did one of the stupid HomeboundHero breathing exercises until the taste of metal cleared her mouth.

This better not make her late.

She opened her eyes again. She was fine. This was fine. There were even handrails. Benny stripped efficiently to her leg and dog tags, then unbuckled the leg. Balancing awkwardly, she nestled it in the *Tools (inbound)* bin—a shallow, slatted metal box that reminded her of the utensil baskets from KP duty—and tapped it shut.

She'd get used to it. She'd have to.

The promised scrubs were in a matching cramped chamber on the other side, along with cushioned booties and flimsy compostable mycelial-web underwear. Graeme was waiting in the hall, doing something Benny couldn't see on her HUD. Whatever it was, she was moving fast, swinging her arms and pivoting her body. Benny waited to be noticed.

"Just a second," Graeme muttered. "There we go."

She dismissed whatever she was looking at with a gesture Benny didn't recognize from the standard interface. But of course, Graeme needed modified commands.

And now, Benny did too.

Graeme's lined face folded back into her usual smile.

"Sorry about that. Minor bot-cleaning kerfuffle in sector C. Nothing serious. Let's get you settled."

Benny's cubicle was spacious, with a round bubble window and room to work sitting or standing, and yet more interactive panels on the wall.

"Drinks come out there. Conveyor bots bring your lunch order. Anything you like as long as it's synth-protein and flavor powder."

"I do love flavor powder," Benny tried. After her tour, that wasn't even really a joke.

Graeme laughed anyway.

"Who doesn't? And out there . . . that's where the magic happens."

The window overlooked a terraced hillside furred with trees too sparse to hide infantry. Off to the right, orderly lines of bots marched in and out, like trails of foraging ants.

"So we're starting you off over there on G44, crew of ten bots." Graeme gestured to an indistinguishable section of hillside. "Three survey-patrol, two for e-waste and complex composites, and one each on metals, silicates, basic organics, complex hydrocarbons including biohazards and inorganic hazmat—heavy metals and radiation, mostly."

The bots were all the same shape, like pointed eggs, but came in a range of sizes and colors: muddy green, white, candy-apple red, cerulean. The ones coming from the hill were smeared with grime. The ones going out shone like new.

"They're level four semi-autonomous?"

Graeme wrinkled her nose.

"Well, they boot level four, but they've got pretty good learning capability, and we never wipe them if we don't have to. Don't be surprised if they exhibit level five or six capacities. Personality, too."

"Really?" Military autos didn't have personality. Too unpredictable.

"Oh yeah. That's where you come in as their handler. It's not just maintenance; you're also providing guidance. They have enough battery to go twelve to eighteen hours autonomous, but they usually need us before that."

Benny leaned her weight on the window ledge. The new leg rubbed, but the outside of her good ankle hurt when she stood too long.

"What kind of guidance?"

"Explosive methane, wildlife, load-bearing furniture, all kinds of stuff. G44 is a fairly old zone, mostly late twentieth and early twenty-first, but because it's peripheral, it's still in the first phase of reclamation. So you're gonna see some, to use the technical term, weird shit."

"Weird shit," Benny repeated.

Graeme laughed.

"Don't worry. Your bots will be on short shifts until you're adjusted. And for now we'll just have you run training modules. We'll go visit decon and recharging later. And speaking of bots needing guidance, friggin' ORG-B17 wants to eat a skunk, so I better skedaddle. Ping me if you need anything!"

When Graeme had gone, Benny dispensed a bulb of seltzer and activated the panel labeled *Chair*. Her leg was still rubbing. She'd shoved blister pads in her pocket on her way out, but her pocket was in her pants and her pants were in a locker.

It was fine. She could sit. It would be fine.

She pulled up the first module. The reclamation bots had mostly the same anatomy as search-and-rescue bots—retractable bucket drums, grippers with claws and spines and rubberized pads, fluid receptacles, cargo compartments, sensors of every imaginable kind. She passed that test on the first try.

The next couple of modules took her through lunch (teriyaki spirulina with udon and sesame FungoNuts) and the discovery that it was a good idea to activate the sunshade on the bubble window at around two. Graeme came back in the middle of the module on manual decontamination, which was an annoying mix of easy (acids neutralize bases) and very difficult (fifty-seven strains of organofluorine-degrading bacteria).

"Everything okay?"

"Yeah! Yeah. Good. I didn't finish the modules but—"

"That's fine. You have two weeks to do them all. Come check out the decon line and then you can shower out and call it a day."

Benny followed her boss, trying not to limp too obviously. As they walked, Graeme pointed out maintenance bays and R&D labs, and Benny met too many people.

They ended up on a steel catwalk. Below, bots were trundling in the gate. She could see the grime on their shiny carapaces better from here: brown organic smudges, scraps of paper and fabric, plastic chips. Most of them, according to the training module, were made of aluminum oxynitride with integrated color. Some had scratches, like healed scars.

"Did you get to the auto decon?"

Benny nodded and recited what she remembered.

"After they drop their payloads, they come here for cleaning. Water with a surfactant, neutralizations for anything the chemical nose IDs, another rinse, then they're air-dried. The water all gets filtered and repurified between uses. Yeah?"

"Pretty much. There are manual decon stations too. Sooner or later you'll have to go scrape something off one of your bots. And their charging bays are down below—we should go see your team's section, show you what I mean about personality."

Graeme paused, glanced down at Benny's leg. "If that's rubbing, my uncle makes really good ointment. Spruce and stuff. I can bring you some."

"I don't want to be a bother."

"No bother. It helped a lot with this old thing, especially when I first got it." Graeme waved her polychrome hand. "I thought the VA had real state-of-the-art stuff now. Synth-skin, motor-assist, neural hookup."

Benny shrugged.

"I didn't want any of that. My mech went down in a cyberattack."

Said like that, it sounded clean. Like the training exercises, or the bots shining from decontamination. Not like the smell of her own sweat and blood cooking in the sun while her leg burned and Jacko screamed in her ear.

Graeme winced.

"Sorry to hear that. Eastern front?"

"Southern."

Graeme winced harder.

"My nephew was on the southern."

Benny nodded.

"Yeah. So . . . I requested an analog leg."

"Makes sense."

Benny shrugged.

Graeme turned her head sharply, looking at an alert on her HUD.

"Shit, I gotta go handle this . . . can you find your way back to the showers okay?"

She waited just long enough for Benny's nod.

Back at her apartment, a package waited in her delivery locker. The return address was in Salmon, Idaho. She'd only ever known one person from Salmon, Idaho. In the elevator, she looked at the ceiling to keep the tears in.

She left the package on the table and sank onto the couch. On her home network, her HUD bristled with notifications.

"Update reentry journal now. You can do it! To access writing coach—"

"Seven missed calls from—Mom! Message from—"

"Reminder—art therapy in—one!—hour and—forty-five! —minutes."

"Continue your—five!—day physiotherapy streak! Always Getting Stronger! Always Getting Stronger trademark of—"

She dismissed them all, unstrapped her leg, and played the block game until the login for art therapy appeared on her HUD. She tapped it and her efficiency apartment disappeared into the VR.

"Start New Project," read one pane. "Load asset packs." "Saved asset packs."

She didn't mind art therapy. She'd picked it off a list of options. It reminded her of drawing with Jacko, but in a good way, not too much. The part where they talked about the art sucked, but most of it was just putting together stuff from the asset packs. Some people in the group made fucked up shit, with distorted bodies and darkness and holes oozing blood. Benny just made landscapes. The biggest asset packs, the photorealistic ones, had scans of all kinds of trees and flowers and rocks. She even recognized one of the mountains from a basic training VR sim; it was the same one Jacko had said looked like a pile of turds. Benny had missed half the targets from giggling.

Benny never used that asset pack.

But mostly, landscapes were okay. She made up stupid little games like "an accurate southeastern landscape" or "an extinct landscape" or "a landscape where everything's blue," with fescue and forget-me-nots and spruce. Except then she had to make up some bullshit about "the bluebird represents healing" and Amy, the facilitator, would nod her avatar head sympathetically, and that asshole Perry's avatar would smirk.

Benny's avatar still had both legs.

Today everything in the landscape was broken. A tree half-killed by lightning, with black bark and green needles around bleach-white wood. A split rock. This weird smeared-sideways flower from one of the asset packs, probably some kind of glitch in the scan, because nothing that freaky could be real. She hesitated over some bugs that reminded her of the bots at work: a shiny round blue-green beetle, a slatey pillbug. Perhaps next week she'd make a round stuff landscape.

She could draw the bots, of course, rather than just relying on what had been scanned into the asset packs.

But there was a lot in the asset packs.

And she hadn't picked up her pencils since she got back.

At the end of class, she didn't have to talk because Brett started crying about his dad's old Mustang—a car, not a horse. That was fine with Benny. She had nothing to say.

It was too late to make dinner, so she ate some seaweed chips and jerky and a granola bar. She didn't even need to shower, she figured. She showered twice a day at work.

She played the block game for a while and went to bed.

She could open that package tomorrow.

The next morning she overslept and nearly missed the shuttle. At work, there was a jar in her internal mailbox labeled "Uncle Bernie's Special Salve," which made her smile.

The rest of the week disappeared into training modules and shadowing other bot handlers. She watched through her HUD while Tark told his gray silicate bot to run a radioactivity scan on some beads, and while Braith guided one of her black survey bots out of a partly collapsed bed frame. Benny passed quizzes and made stilted conversation with her coworkers. Uncle Bernie's salve seemed to help.

The package sat on the counter. It was a busy week.

The next week, she started running her team for a couple of hours at a time, first with Graeme looking over her shoulder, then with her on call. Each bot had its own panel on her HUD, plus the ones for the other bots in the area and overall status alerts—thunderstorms, gas alerts, wildlife sightings, seemed like there was always something going on. It was almost like piloting the mech, except with nothing locked around her body. Just information flowing through and occasional chatter on her headset. Almost like old times.

She made the "round things" landscape in art therapy, with pillbugs and ladybugs and cacti and beach pebbles and fat winter birds. Snarky Perry said it made no biological sense. Brett thought it was cute, and wondered if roundness represented integrity and wholeness.

"Sure," Benny told him. Why not?

The following week, all her training modules were done. It was just her and the bots. She had to ping Graeme with a question almost immediately—was this butterfly in a glass dome the kind of thing she should have a bot dig out for the museum?—but Graeme didn't seem to mind. The salve really did help.

On Tuesday, she opened the package. There was a note, scribbled on a sheet of AlgaWeave:

Dear Benny,
Jacko would have wanted you to have this.
Hoping it brings back good memories.
You're always welcome here in Salmon.
Don't be a stranger.
Love,
Margaret

Benny crumpled the note, then immediately tried to smooth it back out again. Jacko had talked about her mom all the time: the quilts, the spoon collection, the unexpected dirty jokes. A couple times, she'd gotten care packages of molasses spice cookies to share with the squad.

This care package was a sketchbook.

It was like something from the wrong asset pack dropped into her apartment. The black fiberpack cover, ring binding, and FurySaurus sticker were all horribly familiar.

Benny's sketchbook had been decent, with long-fiber creamy AlgaWeave, but Jacko's was the real deal: thick cotton paper. She had thought Jacko was bullshitting the first time she told her to go ahead and draw something on one of those precious pages, but no, that was just Jacko. If Benny flipped through it, about a quarter of the drawings would be her own.

She didn't flip through it.

She put it carefully in a drawer, with Margaret's smoothed note on top.

Then she dismissed all her notifications and played the stupid block game until she was tired enough to sleep.

Her fifth week on the job, Graeme told Benny that her squad had a below-average adverse incident rate. Benny choked up a little. It was nice, maybe, to know she was keeping them safe.

On an uneventful Tuesday, something tripped an alarm. The notification took over her entire HUD, red and flashing, with an urgent beep.

"ENEMY SIGHTED! ENGAGE Y/N?"

She froze, ready to—no, that wasn't right. She blinked, hard.

It actually said, "WARNING: MET-A28 PAYLOAD ERROR."

Payload error? Okay. Payload error. That had been in one of the training modules. Sometimes the reclaimed materials they were dumping got stuck.

She minimized the notification, pulled up the metal bot's interface panel and tapped "Payload purge cycle." Through the front-facing camera, she watched it bank off the track and dock with the hopper. "Purge cycle complete! Continue to decon?"

"Continue," she signaled, watching the minimized error.

It didn't go away.

Instead, the screen turned redder: "REPEAT WARNING: MET-A28 PAYLOAD ERROR."

Something was really stuck in there. That was okay. Manual decon. She'd passed that quiz.

Eventually.

She directed the bot to a manual decontamination bay and set off.

MET-A28 met her in bay C-34, a narrow space with a counter on one side stocked with gloves, wipes, containers, and a lot of nozzles. The blue bot was still, but the lights in its sensors were flickering. When she approached, it beeped sullenly.

Benny hadn't actually seen them in person, she realized. Not up close.

Up close, the bots were big. Waist high at least, and Benny wasn't short. The problem was obvious: one of its grabbing arms was still extended, locked around something shiny. Carefully, Benny moved closer. It was a flat piece of metal, plain silver, barely thicker than her retro ID badge. Narrow, and wider at both ends. A wrench. A very simple one, not adjustable, just a bracket on one side and a loop at the other. More like a wrench icon than an actual tool.

Benny pulled the bot's menu back up, watching in case it moved.

"Cycle arms," she tapped, then jumped as one of the grabbers extended next to her prosthetic. She pressed back against the counter. She could get up onto it if she needed a more defensible position—which was ridiculous. This was a civilian bot. She was a civilian person. Everything was fine.

The arms cycled, grabbing and pinching and scooping, then retracted. All except one. Was the thing stuck in there? Without taking her eyes off the bot, Benny groped around on the countertop for PPE.

"Come on, drop it," she said, locking her gloved fingers around the wrench. It was really jammed in there. She wriggled it, careful not to misalign the arm.

MET-A28 beeped, then beeped again, sounding almost plaintive. Which was silly. It was a bot.

"Give it!" she said, tugging. The bot beeped once more as the wrench finally came loose. It was light as well as thin. Aluminum, maybe, or an alloy. "Okay." She pulled up the menu again and cycled the arms. This time, it retracted properly.

Right. Fine. Weird, but fine.

She set the wrench in a containment tub on the counter and turned around to take off her sweaty gloves. She should file the incident report while she had the object's measurements handy.

In her peripheral vision, something moved. Benny spun to face the enemy. Except the stupid prosthetic didn't pivot properly and her balance deserted her. She went down with a yelp, clipping her hip and shoulder against the counter and hitting the ground hard.

MET-A28 was holding the wrench again.

And the decon bay was too small. She was trapped between the bot and the wall. Her leg didn't work. Benny could feel her pulse speeding up. She tasted blood.

With an effort, she smacked the "Call supervisor" button on her HUD.

She was almost okay when Graeme arrived. She'd made it to the bench across the hall from the manual decon bay, and maybe didn't look too much like she was about to puke.

Graeme sat down next to her and looked straight ahead.

"What happened?"

"It wouldn't let go of that wrench. And then when I finally got it to, it picked it up again." Benny looked at the floor. The scrub bootie stretched weirdly around her plastic foot. She'd probably get fired now.

"Ah. Hang on."

Graeme stood up, walked over to the decontamination bay, and pulled a chemical nose out of one of the drawers. She swabbed the wrench, looked at the readouts, and then sprayed some foam onto it. She was talking to the bot, too quietly for Benny to hear.

"Let's give that a second to work. And then, I think it's time we paid a visit to the charging bays."

Benny frowned.

"Why? What's it doing?"

"It's easier to show you than explain. Let's get this puppy cleaned up first."

Together, they rinsed off the foam and sprayed down the rest of the unit, then checked fresh chemical sniffer results. Through it all, MET-A28 clung to its shiny wrench.

"Okay, tell it to go recharge."

Benny tapped the icons on the HUD menu, and the bot started to move. Benny turned to follow it.

"No, we'll take the elevator. This way. You feeling better now?"

"Yeah. Sorry."

"Nothing to be sorry about. Should've done this week one."

The elevator started descending with a jerk. For a moment, it seemed very small. Benny concentrated on Graeme's prosthetic hand, tapping on the rail. Graeme didn't look worried.

The elevator dinged again. The doors opened.

"After you," said Graeme.

According to the HUD, the bay they were looking for was to the right. The hallway was dark, with pale concrete floors and blue metal gateways punctuating its length. Sensor lights flickered on as they walked, but the bays remained dark. Benny could make out faint red and yellow charging lights in some of them.

They turned a corner, then hit the right number.

Graeme leaned past Benny and poked a panel on the wall. The charging bay lit up.

Benny didn't say anything.

It was going take her a while to figure out what to say.

There were ten alcoves around the room, sized for the different bots. They slept—charged, they weren't alive—nose-in, with their pointed ends tapped into the power supply and their round backs facing the room.

No two alcoves were the same.

One had a curling design of green and blue glass stuck to the wall above it. One had a canopy of wood fragments woven through with long-dead flowers. A small one, with a sensor bot tucked into it, bore lines etched into the wall, arranged into designs that looked almost like pictures.

And one alcove had a sunburst of flat, shiny metal.

"What *is* it?"

"We're not really sure. Almost all of them do it from pretty early in the real-world portion of their training. We tried taking it away, but performance craters. If we reprogram them not to do it, they can't sort the materials right. We even had a couple of digital ethologists from the university come study them."

"And?"

"Their final report was all about bowerbirds collecting blue objects and bees following ultraviolet markings on petals. Best I could tell, it boiled down to 'the bots think it's pretty, and maybe that helps them understand their jobs.'" Graeme shook her head. "I'm sorry. I should've told you, it just slipped my mind. When a bots finds a decoration for its nest, we just let it do its thing."

There was a beep from the hall. Benny was probably imagining things, but it sounded timid. The big blue metal reclamation bot was still holding the silver wrench in its extended arm.

Graeme pulled Benny aside. They stood in front of the charging bay with the glass curlicues while MET-A28 rolled in, rotated, and extended a small nozzle. One of its solvent jets, Benny realized. It pivoted from side to side, probing the air, then poked the nozzle into the gap between a fish knife and a flattened beer can. It sprayed the wall, retracted the nozzle, and pressed the wrench into the sticky patch. Then, it retracted its arm, rolled backwards, beeped once, and rolled forward onto its charging brackets. An orange indicator light lit up on its rear.

"Told ya," Graeme said, "personality."

She shrugged.

Benny shook her head.

"That's so weird."

Graeme shrugged again.

"Like I said, it's just how they make sense of it all."

❧

On the way home, Benny watched the scrubby regenerated forest around the landfill give way to orchards and solar arrays, and then housing developments with orderly palms and oleanders around their gates. She got off at the Caladan Avenue station, where unruly nasturtiums overflowed out of chipped concrete urns, and went back to her apartment.

Her pencil case was where she'd left it when she unpacked.

She went back into the other room and pulled Jacko's sketchbook out of the drawer.

When Mom had helped her set this place up, she'd put a comfy chair in front of the window. Benny shoved laundry off it, sat down, and opened the sketchbook.

There was the dorm at Benicia. On the next page, a seagull with a crab in its beak. A water bottle, casting a long shadow in the afternoon sun. The extended gun-arm of a mech. She flipped through page after page of drawings, some swift, bare lines, some slow and carefully colored in. She found the first of her own drawings, a sailboat in the bay. Jacko had added a mermaid swimming in its wake.

The drawings ended three quarters of the way through the book.

Jacko would never fill those pages.

But new images had started crowding the blank pages of Benny's life. She knew how she'd sketch them. The bots. Graeme's plastic hand. The curvilinear forms of nasturtiums. Mom positioning furniture. The memory of Jacko's face. Benny could see them, rayed out like the bots' mosaics.

Benny bit her lip, pulled a pencil out of the case, and began to draw.

J. L. Rifkin is an author and scientist living in Toronto with two cats, numerous spiders, and one historian. Their fiction has appeared in *Roses & Wildflowers* and *On Spec*, and their nonfiction has appeared in *Molecular Ecology* and *Philosophical Transactions of the Royal Society B*.

The fiction is usually more fun.

The Fighting Youth Is the Most Beautiful

Roseline Mgbodichinma

Roseline Mgbodichinma is the author of *A Body In Spice*. Her writing explores the intricate relationships between nature, womanhood, emotion, bodies, and desire. She is an alumna of the Library of Africa and The African Diaspora (LOATAD) West African Writers Residency programme. She enjoys taking photos and admiring the beauty of nature. Her work has been published in *Isele Magazine*, *Brittle Paper*, *A Long House*, Duke University Press, *North Dakota Literary*, *Tampered Press*, *jfa Human Rights Journal*, *The Willowherb Review*, *Agbowo*, and *SprinNG*, among others. She blogs at www.mgbodichi.com

Photo credit: Nipah Dennis.

Herkimer Inquiries

Rath Mercury

I watched the clip again: the lifeless body of a white-winged dove entered the shot at the top of my screen and plummeted off the bottom a half second later. Whoever was holding the camera didn't notice; they stayed focused on a white guy speechifying about City plans for a soccer stadium. A few seconds later, four or five more birds fell behind the guy at the podium. The audio caught a few gasps from the crowd. But most people were too focused on the foreground to notice what was happening in the background. Observation bias is hilarious.

Next, a lot of birds fell all at once. Probably three dozen. The camera jerked to the ground, catching their bodies scattered like popcorn on the pavement. Off-screen, the speaker continued his endless list of thank yous. The doves did not move again.

Birds falling from the sky mean nothing but bad news—we've known *that* since Roman times. But I still didn't know why a City employee named Heather had sent me this clip in the first place.

I'm Max Herkimer, psychogeographic investigator, or, as I'm more commonly and less charitably called, "that wacko". Heather said she got my number from one of the letters I have a bad habit of sending to various City departments. That particular letter was about renaming a street to pacify an angry genius loci (I mean, can you blame it? No one wants to be the spirit of *Corporate Forest Drive.*) All my letters to the City went directly into the shredder, even the normal ones about installing new public bathrooms. Until now.

Heather asked to meet at a nothing bar on the far end of town, to make sure nobody she knew saw us. Of course, Albuquerque's not *that* big. The first person she saw let out a big "Heather! What are you doing here?" and I slid into a booth while they hugged.

I'd never been to this particular bar. It had *vibes*, though. The decor screamed "Be average!" Vinyl beer ads. Peeling laminate bar. TVs mounted on every TV-worthy surface. It smelled like Lysol and fry oil. I'd put money down that the "good bros" in the corner were cheating on their wives with each other. You learn to spot these things in my line of work.

Another part of my work: avoiding notice. Every space has a pattern. Look at churches: you stay quiet. You keep your head down. You don't wander into the fancy part up front. If you can find that pattern, you have power.

At a bar like this one, the pattern says order a light American lager and get lost in your phone. Heather's pal walked off without even seeing me. You're welcome, Heather. Her dark brown eyes were still scanning for acquaintances as she slid into the booth across from me. She was fifty-five, five foot six. An Albuquerque Dukes cap covered her straight black bob.

She eyed me as she swigged her Jack and Diet. "So . . . should I call you Mis—"

"*Mx.* Herkimer, if you insist, but I prefer just Max." I had neither time for nor interest in watching her puzzle out my gender.

"Alright, Max." Heather cleared her throat. "Your letter got my attention. But I'm curious. What exactly is pyschogeographic inquiry?" It rankled, the way she said my name, like an overburdened school teacher scolding a wretched teen. But there was no way I was going to let a City employee slip through my fingers after all this time.

See, Heather worked for the *City*. I worked for the *city*. Our jurisdictions just looked identical on a map, but they were two very different entities. I worked for the land, the graffiti, the spirits, the water, the birds, the people. She worked for the buildings, the policies, the infrastructure, the power. Still, a solid connection with the City would help with my more esoteric investigations.

"I solve problems people have with, you know," I gestured vaguely, "our urban fabric." I ought to work on the elevator pitch.

She snorted. "Sounds like we have the same job."

"But I work for myself. You follow the rules."

"Yeah, about that. Your card said you were licensed, bonded, and insured." She looked at me with that school teacher's look again. "Who licenses psychogeographers?"

"I do," I said. She coughed. I added, "I have very high standards."

She looked at the door. Maybe it was time to try a different tack.

"I am also bonded and insured. By someone else. And registered with the City as a private investigator. License #94792, if you want to look it up." Maybe it was just wishful thinking, but it looked to me like her shoulders relaxed. "So tell me, what can I help you with?"

"You watched the video?"

"Several times," I said.

She surveyed the bar one more time before continuing. "So . . . obviously there's the birds, right? 47 birds just dropping dead behind a press conference."

"The news said it was bird flu."

"It wasn't bird flu. We tested them." She took another sip of her drink. Her hands had started to tremble. "Aside from the birds, it's just *weird* there. Things go wrong, like, *way* too often."

I loved those kinds of spots. "What kind of wrong?"

"It's not any one thing." She paused as the server refilled our water, then started counting incidents on her fingers. "The birds aren't the only dead animals—they turn up constantly. Cats. Dogs. Raccoons. Then there are the floods. This huge trumpet vine pulled down some power lines and electrocuted someone. A dysentery outbreak. The sewer system." She sighed heavily. "You cannot imagine how bad the sewers have been. Calls to poison control. And the neighbors are convinced there's a serial arsonist."

"Where?"

"Romeroville." Heather pulled out a manila envelope. "There's this little park—that's where the video is from." She showed me maps, newspaper articles, charts of City data from the last two years. She let out a breathy laugh. "Nobody takes me seriously."

"I know the feeling," I murmured as I reviewed her documents. Parts of the City develop a bad attitude, a reckless habit, negative vibes, whatever you want to call it. And they don't always get better on their own. The City had their words for this kind of thing: *Condemned. Substandard. Abandoned. Blighted.* I preferred mine: *Haunted. Cursed. Crossed. Vengeful.*

"So what's the goal here?"

Red crept into her tan, freckled cheeks. Heather took another drink from her Jack & Diet. "I need you to un . . . curse it."

"Might not be cursed, but I take your point." I hadn't expected a City employee to be so direct.

She grimaced and signaled for the check. "Look, I can pay you. But I have to put you down as an exterminator or something."

I had a couple rules in my line of work, but the first was I didn't take clients who were embarrassed to talk to me. Plus, my spidey senses were telling me that something was off with Heather's story. But here's the thing: I was going to be in Romeroville ASAP no matter if I formally took the job or not. A neighborhood so fucked up that birds were falling from the sky? I had a professional obligation to uphold and personal curiosity to satisfy. May as well get paid while I was at it.

And besides—I spent so much time trying to get the City to listen, and now the City had finally come knocking. Rules were made to be bent, right?

"Well, Heather," I said, the same school teacher way she'd said

Max earlier. She blinked. "I'll take the case."

"Great." She slid the papers across the table to me. "And don't call me; I'll call you."

I rolled my eyes.

The next day, the bus wheezed to a stop two and a half blocks from the epicenter of the issues and I stepped into the already hot, dry morning air. I tucked my mop of hair (currently green and pink) into a baseball cap and adjusted the hem of my Lobos t-shirt.

My first time in a new area, I tried to be as invisible as possible. To be clear: I love the city. I love being out in the city. I love looking the way I do. But. As a very obviously queer person, and I do mean that in both the rainbow and the oddball sense, acting weird in a new part of town only invited trouble. Invisibility is a prime protection. Once I got comfy, *then* I'd get weird.

At first glance, Romeroville was a modest residential neighborhood. Public elementary school. Siberian elms and white oaks for shade. Mixed income housing. Nice, wide sidewalks, but not a lot of pedestrians. Dogs barked as I passed. Thunderheads loomed over the volcanoes west of town, promising monsoon rain, but then, they'd been promising that all summer long.

The heart of the trouble was this park. Sometimes what looks supernatural is mundane. But I could tell from two blocks away that this case was not your everyday bit of trouble. If the neighborhood were a mattress, that park was a bowling ball plopped in the middle. All the energy in the area rolled down to that spot.

It wasn't a park in the way a person might imagine a *park*. It was more like an oversized alley, a pedestrian thoroughfare connecting two streets. The cement had been colored blue to look like a river. A brown metal sign read *Acequia Grande Park*. Young honey locusts—what I think of as "new City trees"—shaded the area.

Across the street from the park rose a colorful, fiberglass statue. Sort of a Pietà thing—a man holding a dying woman. They rested on top of a giant hill made of more blue cement, like a mountain or a frozen waterfall. I'm no art critic, but the guy looked bummed out. Beyond the sculpture was a grassy area with a surprising number of informational signs.

I'd read those later. Now that I'd acquired a general lay of the land, I needed to find the more subtle patterns. My methods included talking to strangers, whether human, bird, tree, or other. Observing the swirl of dirt in the wind. Searching the historical record for unusual events. Watching neighborhood cats at work. But the primary tool of a psychogeographer was and always would be the *dérive*: a walk with no destination beyond knowledge of the place itself. (I subscribed to the Situationist *dérive*. Earlier versions involved a lot of opium.)

I found a spot a few blocks from the park where I felt no skin crawling, no heebie-jeebies (yes, that's a technical term). I opened an app to track my path through the neighborhood (Without uploading my location to the cloud. Obviously.)

Then, I began the *dérive:* I wandered, meandered, crept, rushed, paused. I sniffed and inhaled and sang. I closed my eyes. People are always surprised how much shit they miss because they were too busy looking. This is the part where people will start to call the cops on me if I'm not careful.

As I went, I recorded a cluster of sensations. Anything spooky, strange, or generally interesting got a pin on my app:

- Whiff of spring flowers (lilac?) long out of bloom: Pin.
- Footsteps sound hollow on the sidewalk: Pin.
- Skin crawling on the back of my neck: Pin.
- Seven quarters lined up on a fence, all face down: Pin.
- Cold spots: Pin. Pin. Pin. (*Ghosts?*)
- Sound of rushing water, no obvious source: Pin. Pin. Pin.
- Intense encounter with a man who shouted, "You and I share a cousin in Pueblo, Colorado, Miss Miller!" at me. Not my name, but whatever: Pin.

And so I went until about 10 am. I was starving and sweaty. I had 73 pins on my map. But no answers.

Time to get a theory going. I found a bench in the shade and pulled out a peanut butter and red chile sandwich. As I ate, I reviewed the map. A rough outline emerged, of where the strangeness was happening, but that just confirmed what I already knew. Next, I coded the pins based on sight, smell, sound, feel. Sound and smell clustered right down the center of the alley and headed west. Interesting. Visual and touch pins were scattered all over the map.

Alright, Herkimer, think: someone could have cursed this

intersection. But who and why? The only idea I had was that unhelpful note to myself: *Ghosts?* I'd seen solo ghosts over the years, of course. But the sheer *number* of cold spots, the general sense of malevolence in the area, not to mention dropping a bunch of birds out of the sky in the middle of the day . . . it would take a lot of ghosts to do that. Like, *piles* of 'em. I'd never seen something like this. Not even in that abandoned hospital.

Seemed unlikely, but maybe there had been some kind of horrific tragedy I'd missed? Amelia would know.

"Special Collections Library, Ms. Collier speaking."

"Hey, Amelia."

"Max! Too busy to come in person?" Amelia was head librarian at Special Collections, the archival home of everything about the City *and* the city. The perfect library—a relic of a different time, full of Albuquerque oddities, and deeply haunted. Plus the librarians *loved* me. I always had research-y questions instead of "What's the code for the bathroom?"

"You know I'd rather be there." I imagined her behind the desk, in a knee-length floral dress, gray cardigan, and chunky Mary Janes. She always looked professional, but I knew for reasons I shall not disclose that she hid a number of excellent tattoos under that sweater.

She laughed. "What are you working on this time?"

"I'm in Romeroville."

"Ooh, nice. Not the oldest neighborhood around, but pretty close. It grew up in Colonial times—should be some signs about it."

Yes, yes, *I know*. Everybody always says, "Read the signs!" and I'm over here like, *Why do you think I'm staring at this ant colony?*

Anyway, it was cool history but way too early. "What about more recently, like the last couple years? I'm looking for something that would," I paused, failing to think of a different way to say it. " . . . make a lot of ghosts." Amelia didn't really *believe* in my weird shit, but she also didn't laugh at me. Usually.

She snorted. But just a little. "Are you talking, like, a mass murder? I thought you didn't do the whole true crime thing."

"I don't, but yeah, something like that. Or a gruesome accident? Old folks' home burned down? Horrific school bus crash or something?" I sounded stupid, but I was trying to get the scale of the thing across to her.

"Not seeing anything like that." I could hear her mouse clicking. "It's a pretty quiet place."

"Dammit." I chewed my lip and stared at the alley. Back to square one. Ghosts would have been a hard sell for Heather, but at least I'd had a theory.

"I've never known someone to get so morose that an old folks' home didn't get burned down," Amelia said.

"Sorry—that's not it. I just . . . there's something weird going on here."

"You know I'm a born skeptic. Not much help with ghosts. But the other thing about that neighborhood is they really—pardon my language—fucking hate the City."

Huh. Heather hadn't mentioned that little detail. "Oh, yeah?"

"It's been a whole thing. The City let the feds put two freeways through it in the 60s. Then in the 70s, the City tried to declare it substandard, so they could put in some government buildings, and Romeroville organized themselves to stop all that. *Then* there was a Superfund site that was 'cleaned up' in the 90s. Anyway, probably nothing to do with your ghosts, but figured I'd mention." I could hear her addressing a patron. "Hey, Max, sorry—gotta go. Call me back later?"

"No worries. Tell you about it over drinks on Friday."

Was this City nonsense related to the birds dying? Unclear. But was it fishy as hell that Heather hadn't mentioned it? Absolutely.

Heather answered my third call, her voice low. "I told you not to call me."

"Hi, *Heather*," I said. "Curious if you were planning to tell me about the whole *Romeroville hates the City* angle of the case."

"Let me get outside." Her footsteps echoed down a stairwell.

I skimmed the informational signs as I waited. These people were serious. They had a *committee*. A crest for their committee. A timeline of their protests. I let out a low whistle. "Man, they really do hate you guys. Sounds like maybe you earned it though."

She huffed. "Yes, there have been . . . tensions. Obviously. But that was a long time ago. Are you saying you think this is *our* fault?"

"Do *you* think it's your fault?"

"I didn't think all that was relevant."

I took a deep breath. Where to start. "Heather, you mean well. But there are things in this world you don't know much about. Shit can get weird. Right now, things are getting bad in Romeroville." And I was getting angry. "So is there any other information you're withholding?"

An indignant breath came over the phone. "Okay, fine. There are plans to build a soccer stadium there. They asked me to find out about the neighborhood. See if I could make the neighbors a little more receptive to our plans. Like, in a good way, you know."

"Everybody *loves* being made more receptive," I muttered.

"Point is I noticed all this bad shit happening there. But the funders didn't care. If anything, it made them more excited. They thought if the neighqbors got spooked, they'd let the City have the land." She huffed again. "Well, it worked, for what that's worth. A little too well. Some of the local funders got spooked, too, and now they're backing out."

Say what you will about New Mexicans, but I have always loved the way we as a people take weird shit seriously. Still, what did I have to do with any of this? Why had she called *me* to fix it? Nobody in the City respected me. The only thing calling me would achieve was discredit—Oh. *Oh*.

"Okay, I get it. You called me because you knew that if *I* started talking about how it was haunted, nobody would take it seriously. They'd be too embarrassed to be associated with me and my weird theories." Tears pricked my eyes. "And your stadium would be back in business."

Heather didn't say anything. I'd learned to read silences over the years and this one was loud and clear. *Goddammit*. I'd been so excited they were taking me seriously for once that I'd broken my own rules.

"Even though you hired me for bullshit reasons, you do still have to pay me." My voice was tight. I hung up.

The sun beat down on me as I stood alone in Romeroville. My instincts had warned me something was off and I was pissed I hadn't listened. I took a deep breath and listened to the sounds of the city around me: traffic on the major arteries, sure. But also the skittering sound of a lizard in the leaf litter under a golden currant bush. Children shrieking at recess. And a westerly wind blowing the clouds nearer. Beneath it all, that malevolent energy roiled.

I didn't have to help Heather any more. But I definitely wanted to know what was going on in Romeroville. The neighbors ought to have some insights.

A woman, graying hair pulled into a bun, watered roses in the shade of her yard. She had an eye on me but pretended she didn't. The piney scent of rosemary wafted through the air. Her garden, ringed by a straw-flecked adobe wall, bordered the Acequia Grande and was exuberant with lavender, blue flax, and orange globe mallow.

"Lovely garden," I called as I approached. "Can't get my roses to look like yours no matter how hard I try." It was the truth. I'd tried everything and they were still scraggly.

"I have my secrets." She stood several feet from the gate, hands clasped behind her. Not quite ready to trust me. "But if I told you, I'd have to kill you."

I nodded gravely. "Otherwise my roses might beat yours at the State Fair."

She smiled. "Couldn't have that."

We were both quiet for a moment, but she didn't move to go inside.

"I heard the City wants to build a soccer stadium here," I said.

"They do." I could see her clocking my outfit, deciding which side I was on. I was real glad I'd chosen the university t-shirt and not the soccer team t-shirt for today's invisibility drag.

"Do you know where, exactly?"

She gestured broadly, a furrow in her brow. I frowned sympathetically.

"Sorry for all the questions, but have you noticed anything strange lately?" It can be awkward, trying to explain what a psycho-geographic investigator does, but I've learned that, at least in New Mexico, if you ask the weird question first, you get a lot of information. Some of it is even useful. "I heard about all those birds that died. Stuff like that?"

She gave me another look, and I swear I could almost read her thoughts. But maybe that was just my imagination getting away from me. In place of an answer, she asked, "Would you like some water? Or lemonade? Hot day to be walking around."

"Lemonade sounds great." I paused. "My name's Max."

"Lupe. Nice to meet you, Max."

The aggressive atmosphere of the neighborhood dropped away as I crossed into her yard. We sat on her porch as we drank the lemonade, which was sweet and strong. She had sprinkled dried lavender on top. When she spied the colorful hair under my ball cap, she insisted I take the hat off so she could admire my messy mop. A long broomstick skirt colored like red clay pooled around her wrinkled, brown feet, toenails painted sky blue. She told me a little about her gardening secrets and her grandchildren. I told her about my pet squirrel—a rescue. Condensation dripped from my glass and cooled my foot. I wondered if she'd ever answer my question, but I also kind of didn't mind that she hadn't. What good is life as a psychogeographic investigator if you can't have lemonade with strangers on a hot day?

Then she finally turned back to it. "I've been here for, oh, forty years. Not quite as long as some. Best place I've ever lived. But something in the land isn't quite right. I do my best with this little patch of dirt. But it's *sad*, no?"

Sad. I'd been feeling the vibes all wrong. The air was filled with rage, yes, but it was the rage that comes from grief.

"It is," I said and we looked at each other. I decided then that I'd figure this out for Lupe's sake, even if nobody else cared.

"Thanks for the lemonade." I lifted my empty glass to her in a toast.

Lupe nodded like she, too, had decided something, then disappeared into the house. When she returned, she pressed a book about roses into my hands, the edges frilled with sticky notes. I put the book in my bag, tucked my hair back into my cap, and promised I'd return soon.

Back at Acequia Grande Park, the epicenter, I couldn't believe I'd missed the grief, the helplessness in the air. I'd been too focused on Heather's version of events. Now, I paced the length of the park, feeling echoes of my morning observations: cold spots, whispers with no obvious source. Back in the sun, sweat ran down my neck into the channel of my spine. A handful of white-winged doves landed nearby to drink from a puddle. The blue sky had gone grey while we chatted, and the trees worried themselves sick in the wind. I hoped—and could feel everything around me, from the sidewalk to the bumblebees, hoping as well—that today there would be rain.

Okay. Not ghosts. And, though I *was* pissed at Heather, this didn't feel like a case of the City neglecting a neighborhood. Yeah, the stadium idea sucked. But this had been going on a lot longer than that.

As I walked, I let my focus go soft. Heat radiated from the blue pavement river, blurring the edges of my vision. I imagined the years peeling away. Back to the 70s when it was declared "substandard." Back to the agricultural 1800s. Time grew thin. If I squinted, I could see (or imagine?) the area as it had been: sheep grazing. Water flowing where I stood, through the acequia the park was named after: an irrigation channel carrying water from the Rio Grande. These ditches spiderwebbed the area, carrying the green life of the river just a little farther into the surrounding desert.

Acequias were easy to miss. Some were well kept, some less so. And in Romeroville? Paved over. Just then, the drinking doves exploded in flight, breaking the spell. My shoulders tensed.

One small feathered body remained, convulsing on the edge of the water. I walked over to it. The other birds landed overhead on a power line, witnessing me as I picked the creature up. Its body trembled in my palm, so light it was like the air itself was seizing. Before I could think what to do, it stopped shivering and died.

The birds took flight again, noisy and chaotic. I traced the line of their passage. Never ignore the communications of a bird. They landed on the statue, perched on the mass of blue that looked like the headwaters of a spring. A spring capped with a man cradling a dying woman. *The water is lost.* I realized I was standing right about where they'd had the press conference I'd seen on the video clip.

I looked down at the bird in my hand, at its bright orange, sightless eye. A trash can stood nearby, but putting a messenger in the literal garbage was a quick way to get on nature's bad side. No. I needed to bury the bird.

I didn't pay much attention when I heard someone shout, "Him!" It's not a word I hear applied to me very often, so I kept scanning the ground, searching for a suitable avian burial site,. But then I heard footsteps. A moment later, a heavy hand fell on my shoulder and spun me around.

The man it belonged to snarled at me, red-faced in his rage. My shock garbled his words, mixed them up until I couldn't put them back together. My shoulders rose along with my hands and forearms, to shield me and the bird, the little thing, lifeless against my thumping heart.

He grabbed the collar of my shirt and pulled me back to that spot where all the bad energy pooled. Did he realize that's what he was doing? I stumbled after him, and the jumble of noise coming from his mouth resolved into words: "I already called the cops, you prick."

I had no idea what he thought I'd done but—*Ah.* He pointed at a car with all four tires slashed.

Something I've noticed over the years: I pretty much only ever get identified as a *guy* when people are pissed at me. I accelerated to match his pace and tucked the point of my elbow into the crook of the arm he was using to drag me. His hand slackened in surprise, and I pressed down with my elbow to twist away from his grasp. Nice move, Herkimer—but I barely had time to preen before he tackled me to the ground. I banged my arm up good as I moved to protect the little feathered body still in my hand.

The hot concrete scraped my cheek as he held my head down. Pulsing rage flooded me. I wanted to fuck this guy up. But that feeling wasn't mine: it was the land, the water, the very earth rising up and egging us on. This guy had 30 pounds on me and (*what the hell was I going to do with this bird*) I was down a hand. I don't like making a scene but, goddammit. I was going to have to.

"Help!" I shouted. I could have pitched my voice up to be more audible, sound more vulnerable, but it felt wrong. "Lupe!"

He was still screaming at me, but I couldn't make sense of the words. I wondered if this rage was as foreign to him as it was to me. A rumble of thunder, low and easy, joined the excitement.

Neighbors were already out in their yards, staring at us. Not every oddball is the center of attention type, no matter how we dress. My cheeks flushed. Tears filled my eyes. My mouth tasted sour. A mineral smell rose from the ground.

I called again. "Lupe! Somebody. Help!" He pushed down, shuddering, and pain throbbed through my temples, my cheek, my jaw. I bucked against him hard, but he didn't move. Still he could have—should have—been hitting me and he wasn't. Something was up.

Everyone, human or otherwise, was in thrall to us—or whatever was using us. Time seemed to flow downhill, pooling around our tableau. The birds moved in closer, knowing I held their kin. The trees grew still and even the sky had gathered itself up. A hot drop of moisture landed on my cheek and ran into my mouth. *The water is lost.* It tasted salty. Sweat? Tears?

Then the rain came. Fat, ice-cold raindrops slapped against leaves, against skin, drumming on cars and roofs. With my face this close to the pavement, my nostrils filled with the smell of evaporating rain water—that mineral smell I'd noticed earlier.

The hammer of rain drops broke the spell; the entire neighborhood seemed to exhale. Time resumed its normal flow as people started to scatter. Another hot drop of moisture—tears, I was pretty sure this time—landed amid the cold ones. The pressure on my head lessened as he sagged off to one side. I rolled away, landing in a cold stream of storm run-off.

The man's rage-torn face was slack now, as if he'd just woken up. I opened my mouth to speak, but a chunk of hail pinged him on the head. Larger and larger pieces of ice bounced on every surface. He shook his head and stumbled away.

I took shelter under the nearest tree, one hand cradling the bird and the other touching the abrasions on my face. I was no stranger to the way rain would lighten the city's mood, but I'd never seen anything like this. The doves rustled and cooed in the tree above me. I tried and failed to calm the shivers that had taken over my body.

Lupe's gentle voice called out to me. "Max!"

She waved from her front porch. I curled my body over the bird and ran to her.

"Are you okay?" She reached for my face. I flinched.

"Yes. No. Sorry. Yes. I was thinking I'd—" I wiped my eyes with my empty hand and held the bird out, feathers mussed. The sight of the feathers out of place turned the shivers into tears. "I was planning to bury this bird, I guess. Before."

She nodded. "What about here, once the rain ends?" She gestured at a tiled *nicho* in her adobe wall. It enclosed a statue of the Virgin Mary, a rosebush flourishing at her feet. People often assume someone like me doesn't go in for Christianity, and for the most part, I don't. But sacred is sacred.

I looked for signs of mockery in her face, but found none. The pressure eased in my heart. At least I'd get one thing right today.

Lupe fetched a compress for my face. I straightened the errant feathers and laid the dove on her porch. We sat in silence as the storm poured off her porch, raindrops illuminated in gold by the coming sunset. Water flooded down that big fiberglass pietà. Both figures wept, and the blue mountain they sat on turned into a waterfall.

Lupe clicked her tongue. "It's gonna be a mess to clean this one up."

I didn't understand at first, but—right. Heather had given me flood records. Hmm. I remembered the sensation from earlier, like the

Acequia Grande was a bowling ball sitting on a mattress. The park must catch all the storm water for the neighborhood. And probably a few neighborhoods beyond.

I stepped off the porch into the drizzle. *The water is lost.* That phrase came back to me as I watched the rain fill the gutters, sheet across the street—and head to the Acequia Grande. I remembered the way that man's pressure on my face had slackened with the first drops of water.

The water is lost. This water shouldn't be flowing over concrete to the sewers. I turned to Lupe. "The way it changed when the rains came. You felt it, too. I know you did."

She held my eyes with a long, level gaze, then nodded. I looked out at the flat pavement of the park, water rushing down it in a pattern that told us everything we needed to know: fast, flat, unnatural. I imagined earth instead of blue-tinted concrete. Natural dips and rises to slow the water, let it soak into the ground. Instead of a few trees trapped in concrete rings, we would have yucca, desert willow, horsetail, screwbean mesquite, and goldenrod thriving where the water collected.

Or: the City could build a stadium. Instead of this small park, we would have acres of blacktop, no shade, and the land disconnected from water and life for good.

Wait. Wasn't that what the press conference had been about in the first place? The stadium? I should have seen it sooner. To fix this one, I was going to have to talk to Heather again. Gross.

The rain stopped and Lupe turned to me. "Shall we? The ground will be soft."

She watched in silence as I tucked the bird's fragile body into the earth, then covered it in soil and bark.

"Most people don't care enough to bury a city bird." Lupe held up her garden hose. "Want a rinse?"

I stuck my hands out. She hit the trigger on the sprayer, gently, and cool water rinsed the dirt from my hands. The flock of white-winged doves cooed mournfully from their nearby post.

I met Heather for the second time at a bar of my choosing: a windowless poolhall in the heart of downtown. It smelled of stale beer and incense. The music on the jukebox was loud and aggressive. I hadn't forgiven her for using me to discredit her opponents and I wasn't going to put up with her shitty bar this time.

Once again, Heather carried a Jack and Diet from the bar.

"What happened to your face?" she asked.

"Not your business," I answered. "Speaking of business, though, I found your culprit."

I walked her through it: the acequia was abandoned in 1976. The earliest sign of weirdness was in 1977, when the neighborhood finally had access to the City's drinking water and didn't want to bother with irrigation any longer. The land was lonely, heartbroken for water. But that probably would have been fine. It was when the City announced plans to build a soccer stadium that shit had gotten real. Whatever spirit animated that place didn't want to be buried in a parking lot. And it wasn't going down without a fight.

To Heather's credit, her first question wasn't "Are you stupid?" It was "What are my options?"

"Either way you're gonna have to find somewhere else for the stadium. But, since you asked. Option one: rebuild the old acequia. But there's a lot more city between Romeroville and the river these days. Even if you took it underground . . . . " I sucked air through my teeth. "It's gonna cost."

Heather blanched. I had to guess she was imagining the many, many, *many* buildings, properties, roads, and parks involved. Precisely the feeling I wanted her to have so *my* idea didn't sound so hard.

"Option two: turn the Acequia Grande park into a rain garden. You'll stop having all these weird incidents, which is what I care about. The flooding will stop, which is what the neighbors care about."

She gave me a flat look. "What am I supposed to tell the people who want the stadium? *The thirsty land is killing people?*"

"Obviously not. That's the kind of shit I say. You get an engineer to say you need higher ground. The monsoons happen at the height of the United season. Blah blah blah."

She looked at me for a long time, then the corners of her mouth curled up. "Putting in a rain garden would be a big PR win."

As if I cared. I checked my watch. Just enough time to walk to the bar where I was meeting Amelia. "Done and dusted. Can't say it's been a pleasure. You'll get my bill this week."

I headed out into the twilight: a couple hurried into a ramen joint. A lowrider cruised past, done up in rose gold and purple. Heat rose from the sidewalk. The stars were beginning to shine and Amelia was waiting for me. A perfect night in my city.

One year later, almost to the day, I was back in Romeroville in the pink light of dawn. The park didn't look so different: the same shape, trees, benches. But now instead of broad swathes of blue cement, the paths were narrowed, made of water-permeable materials. The ground was shaped and carved, not so differently than I'd imagined, and the plantings Lupe and I had done were starting to look hearty.

Two cottontails darted under a bush as Lupe, Amelia, and I approached. The City would have their opening ceremony later that day. I wanted to do a ceremony of our own first.

I closed my eyes, felt for that bowling ball on a mattress sensation. It had changed; the energy in the neighborhood flowed easily through the park. We had all collected rainwater, a gallon or so each, just for this. I opened my eyes and found Amelia looking at me with an arched eyebrow and a smile. I directed her and Lupe to opposite corners of the park, and we poured out our rain water with all the solemnity we could muster. I watched it sheet across the ground and soak in as the first rays of sun broke over the mountain. I whooped and the other two joined me, raucous and loud as roosters.

Wasn't much, but it felt right. As for what the land thought, I had to trust we'd done okay.

We watched the City ceremony from Lupe's porch. Well, sort of. The speeches were quite boring and I wanted to show Amelia an antlion in Lupe's yard.

Heather came over after the fuss was done. "I know I messed up. But if you're looking for work . . . . " She handed me a thumbdrive. "Give me a call."

Would you look at that? Heather talking to Max Herkimer in public. Could I trust her? Probably not. But I *have* always loved a good mystery. I dropped the thumbdrive in my pocket and headed back toward the house.

A roadrunner, all punk rock eyeliner and jagged crest, ran along the fence beside me and hopped into a willow tree. A blue whiptail lizard dangled from its beak. Storm clouds, ripe and dark, ambled in from the west. The scent of water hung in the air.

RATH MERCURY writes horror, fantasy, romance, poetry, and science fiction, always queer. They have also worked as a choreographer, open source software developer, arts administrator, and more. It's been busy. Mercury lives in New Mexico. When not writing, they play tabletop games and classical guitar. https://www.rathmercury.com

The Main Thing Is to Not Be Afraid: Tove Jansson, Obsessive-Compulsive Disorder and Art in the Era of Climate Change

Moshe Schaffzin

"Everything looks worse in the dark, you know"[1], writes Tove Jansson, famous Finnish painter and children's author, in her first book *The Moomins and the Great Flood* during the last years of World War II. I imagine her sitting hunched over a wooden desk stained with paint and covered in pencil shavings, interrupting her writing every few minutes to glance anxiously out the window at the grey Finnish sky. I see myself in her, as I sit writing on my laptop in Canada where the temperature has reached 31 °C, compulsively picking up my phone to check for some kind of catastrophic emergency alert whenever my mind begins to wander. The scream of an air raid siren and an iPhone sounding the disaster alarm don't sound that different after all.

Though my anxiety is a product of the time in which I live, it is also a product of my obsessive-compulsive disorder, which has been the biggest obstacle for me in all areas of my life for as long as I can remember. I have begun 2025 with another OCD relapse, and my obsessive thoughts, which normally involve fears of terminal illness, have this time been coloured by the effects of a changing climate. Recently, I've been reading a lot about Tove Jansson, partly because I've been interested in her work since I was a child, but also because I've found her to be quite relatable. Like myself, she was both a writer and painter, but what has been grabbing my attention in my self-guided research the most is the fact that she began her professional artistic career in the midst of World War II. Very rarely has humanity faced a level of existential threat similar to that brought by the Second World War, but the largest threat facing humanity at this current instance, climate change—and its resulting environmental, social and political breakdown—does just that.

To quote a cliche, "history doesn't repeat itself, but it does often

1. Jansson, Tove. *The Moomins and the Great Flood*. Translated by David McDuff, Drawn & Quarterly, 2018, p.14

rhyme," and as such I, as a university student just beginning their writing career in the midst of all this, have been looking to Tove Jansson for guidance. By examining both her professional and personal writings, I have come to the conclusion that the only way through the challenges that coincide with climate change is to accept the uncertainty these events bring without avoidance—such as expressed in the typical model for OCD recovery—while still holding onto hope. As demonstrated by Jansson, the medium of art is perhaps the most effective way of processing and channeling all manner of anxieties about the future into beautiful creations that inspire this hope in the midst of existential threat.

The first real memory I have related to OCD takes place when I am six years old. I'm sitting with my elementary school class, learning cursive on the first Wednesday of the month in mid-spring. If you've ever lived in the American Midwest, then you're probably familiar with the ebbing siren that unleashes its guttural, frankly pretty frightening voice whenever the region is bisected by the path of a tornado or nearly swept into the muddy, Ohio River by a severe thunderstorm . . . or if it happens to be a first Wednesday of the month in spring, when they test the alarms. The typical reaction is a brief seizure of anxiety, leopard fur standing on end, before the memory surfaces that yes, today *is* a first Wednesday. There's nothing to worry about, and the conversation lulls back to a dull purring. I wonder how often Midwesterners in the 2020s find themselves in these periods of brief, full-body-encompassing anxiety, and if it ever happens in the absence of alarms.

I'm sitting in class with my teacher, who is helping me learn to perfect my cursive A, when the room momentarily buzzes with anxiety at the ringing of the familiar siren song, before settling back into calm at my realization that it's Wednesday. It has been stormy all day, and little Moshe anxiously twists their Skechered feet in four clockwise circular motions, then four counter-clockwise circular motions. Obsessive-compulsive disorder is a very misunderstood disease that is often stereotyped as being an extreme form of germophobia, but this could not be further from the truth. OCD is characterized by unwanted, intrusive thoughts about a particular "obsession," that is, an extreme personal fear. This can be anything from fear of developing a serious illness to fear of getting into a car accident. To counteract these obsessive thoughts, people with OCD will engage in "compulsions," which are repetitive behaviours that momentarily relieve the anxiety, but that end up reinforcing the obsession and making the anxiety worse in the long run.

My teacher, seeming to have a sixth sense for what would become my obsessive-compulsive disorder says something like, "Don't worry. It's just a Wednesday. There's no tornado." I remember her reassurances bringing me first calm, then an overwhelming anxiety once that immediate relief wore off, as is the case with most reassurances in relation to OCD. First the sweet, falsified comfort, then the tsunami of fear. I have no way of knowing, when the first drop of reassurance calms the swirling whirlpool that was my childhood OCD, that despite it being a first Wednesday, when *real* tornadoes are *never* supposed to happen, a severe thunderstorm will knock down the hundred-year-old oaks in the backyard of my childhood home that very night. At that moment, all I care about is how nice it feels to think, "Yes, it's just a Wednesday," before being yanked underwater by my pigtails again.

In a letter written during the Second World War, Tove Jansson writes:

> You can't scream inside yourself. You push things aside, you keep working, but you avoid things that bring the outer world closer to you: newspapers, radio, the telephone, war magazines. They dig up everything that's smouldering and burning deep inside you. Even though one does not bury one's head in the sand but is intensely present, every moment in, every part of oneself.[2]

One of the principal but lesser known symptoms of obsessive-compulsive disorder is avoidance. It's a form of compulsion where, instead of doing a certain behaviour to relieve the anxiety caused by intrusive thoughts, you avoid things that trigger the intrusive thoughts in the first place. Avoidance is something I have struggled with for as long as I have had OCD. In middle and high school, I refuse to turn in homework assignments, or don't complete them in the first place, because I am scared of getting bad grades. Of course, this means I not only fail the assignment, but am also forced to take home letters to my parents chastizing me for my failure (which I secretly recycle, along with the offending papers marked with a circled or underlined "F"). It doesn't mean the grades aren't there; I still get low Cs or Ds in the classes that make me the most anxious, but OCD is not logical, and neither is my avoidance. But then, the fear itself isn't logical in the

2. Westin, Boel. *Tove Jansson: Life, Art, Words.* Translated by Silvester Mazzarella, University of Minnesota Press, 2024, p.128

first place either. I graduate with a GPA of 3.35, not the best, not the worst, and am still able to get into a major university. My bad grades affect me very little.

But during this most recent relapse, my avoidance has taken on a new form. Starting in January of this year, I have begun avoiding the news. I can't figure out why—the election? Anxiety about my family in the U.S.? Catastrophizing about the various wars happening around the world? I remember one instance of laying on the couch being unable to stop crying, my sobs turning into weak, raspy, hiccuping and my eyes swollen to bee stings, after accidentally seeing a scary news headline on a newspaper stand in downtown Ottawa. "Who even reads newspapers anymore?" I think to myself. "They're inventing headlines to make me upset." From that moment on, I decide that I need to avoid the news. I delete nearly all my social media; I block news websites on my phone; when I walk by a newspaper stand, I look the other direction and try to hold my breath, as if the bad news was a ghost trying to possess me as I passed a graveyard.

When I see a headline about there being more CO2 in the atmosphere today than there ever has been in any year human beings have lived, and I feel the familiar somersault, body-turning-inside-out feeling that typically accompanies seeing a trigger unexpectedly, I realize what it is I've been avoiding: climate change. Unlike my past fears, like my fear of having terminal cancer at 21 with no family history, I find it very hard to recognize this fear as improbable, because it isn't, really: it's happening. Every day, every hour, every minute, I am (and you are) living in a world where the climate is changing—and those changes are happening right now, not in some hypothetical, unlikely anxiety scenario.

The thing about avoidance is that it makes the anxiety worse whenever the avoidant behaviour is engaged in. In your mind, it feels like you're preventing the anxiety because you're avoiding the things that make you anxious, which seems logical. However, even if this provides momentary relief, the object of fear still exists when you're not actively looking at it, so the anxiety about it never wholly leaves. If this is the case, then why is it that so many people spend every day of life in 2025 avoiding thinking about climate change? I can recognize, as someone who has done all manner of intensive OCD treatment, that this is an irrational behaviour. The threat of climate change is there; trying not to think about it doesn't make it not exist, but we keep doing it anyway.

The simple answer is that most people are under the impression that there is nothing they can do to stop climate change, because they're just a little person with no power, so they justify the irrationality of avoiding thinking about the subject by saying, "Well, there's nothing I can do, so it's not worth thinking about." But how healthy a coping mechanism is that really? In my experience, it's not a very healthy one at all. The more time we spend pushing away our fear, the worse it gets, until we reach some kind of mental tipping point where the fear completely takes over. In exposure, response, prevention therapy (ERP), which is the gold standard treatment for obsessive-compulsive disorder, you have to run towards the fear in order to overcome it, because not thinking about the fear doesn't make the threat stop existing.

So if we accept climate change without running away from it, what happens? Often, people's immediate reaction is to fall into despair, as humans are wont to do in times of extreme upheaval. During the war, Jansson writes:

> War everywhere, the whole world at war. What can I say? I don't say very much these days . . . I don't think very clearly either, it's all just feelings. Sometimes it feels as if something of the collected agony of the whole world has been weighing heavily in me like a lump and threatening to burst apart. Never has sympathy been so mixed with bitterness, love so mixed with hate, and the will to live–and despite everything to live rightly and worthily–with an urge to just creep away and let go[.][3]

Feelings of despair are common in obsessive-compulsive disorder. Most intrusive thoughts involve spiraling about what feels like an inevitable tragic event. During the height of my relapse, I often spend over an hour pacing back and forth, ruminating about every way climate change could destroy what I've built so far in my short life. I wonder if people without OCD find themselves acting similarly when thinking about climate change. Maybe not to the same degree, but I imagine many of the people reading this article without OCD have felt the same all-encompassing anxiety response at one point or another.

Often in leftist circles people will talk about how panic isn't helpful, which is true, but even if you can suppress the panic through compartmentalization, the feelings still exist, they just now have no outlet, and the despair still weighs on you heavily. This, I believe, is

3. Ibid., p.130

what leads people to avoid talking about climate change. With no outlet for their feelings and no idea how to move forward, they avoid the thing that makes them anxious, because otherwise they would fall into despair. Avoidance is unhealthy and provokes anxiety, but so does spending time actively pondering what climate change means for you as an individual and for us as a collective. In 1944, Jansson loses her ability to paint.[4] At the time, she is primarily an oil painter rather than a writer.

With no outlet, her despair becomes more pronounced and all-encompassing, her mind overwhelmed by the existential threat of the war. It is also around this time that her mind begins to search for a new outlet for her anxiety: playful children's writing.[5] It is in 1945, during the last months of the war, when it seems that the barbarity of the fighting has reached an unbearable level, that Jansson's first Moomin book, *The Moomins and the Great Flood*, is published.[6]

The conflict in Moomin narratives, especially those written during and immediately after the war, is often driven by true peril. Floods of biblical proportions and world-ending comets are just some of the threats the main characters are faced with. Unlike many other children's narratives, the Moomin characters are allowed to express their fear and sadness openly.

There is one scene in *Comet in Moominland*, likely inspired by the bombing of Helsinki in 1944,[7] where the characters discover that the red-hot comet hurtling towards their valley has made the sea dry up. Snufkin, who is normally the calm, wise, advice-giver of the group, weeps at the sight of the dry seabed.[8] I can't help but be reminded of my own circumstances, in which the town I live in, located in southern Ontario, an area rarely faced with drought, has recently announced strict water restrictions due to dry conditions in the midst of a two-month-long heatwave.

But despite the peril present in these narratives, the stories always end with a beacon, however small, of unbreakable hope. At the end of *Comet in Moominland*, while the characters huddle in a dark cave

---

4. Ibid., p.157

5. Souter, Anna. "Tove Jansson Found Refuge in Play." *Hyperallergic*, Hyperallergic, 21 Nov. 2024, hyperallergic.com/968411/tove-jansson-found-refuge-in-play/

6. Westin, p. 161

7. Ibid., p.167

8. Jansson, Tove. *Comet in Moominland.* Translated by Ernest Benn, Square Fish, 2010, p.118

waiting for the end, the comet suddenly diverts. When they emerge from their bunker, they find the sea rushing back into the dry seabed and laugh with relief as they play in the waves.[9]

What does art like that of Tove Jansson's mean for us, we who are also living through an era of unprecedented change and ecological breakdown? If avoidance only multiplies anxiety and ruminating leads to despair, then maybe the correct way to deal with this overwhelming climate anxiety is to channel it into art. Recently, climate fiction has been emerging as a prominent genre both academically and commercially, with many universities now teaching it as part of their creative writing programs. Climate fiction authors like Octavia E. Butler and Jeff VanderMeer line bookstore shelves across the world. As a writer of primarily climate fiction myself, I may be biased, but it seems to me that there is a real want from the general populace to have an outlet for their climate worries. The common thread I have found between many of the climate narratives I've read, even dark and dystopian ones such as Butler's *Parable of the Sower* or Omar El-Akkad's *American War*, is a small but persistent nugget of hope.

For someone like me with obsessive-compulsive disorder, acceptance of the uncertainty while also having hope is the most important thing for recovery. Nowhere have I found a more effective strategy for coping than in creating art about climate change that expresses all the fears swirling inside me, funnels them into narratives that ground me with feelings of acceptance of my situation, and inspires me with practical solutions for a better future. I hope that the solutions posed by artists and writers can become a vehicle not just for personal acceptance of the reality of climate change, but also for collective implementation of these solutions.

To overcome climate change, we must take a page out of the OCD recovery manual and accept global warming as reality without avoidance while still holding onto hope, however slim it may seem. Art can be a vehicle for our anxiety about both our reality and our hope, and maybe, if accepted by enough people, it can also become a vehicle for positive change within ourselves and in our societies. In *Moominland Midwinter*, Tove Jansson writes, "All things are so very uncertain, and that's exactly what makes me feel reassured."[10] An era of changing climate has now become inevitable, but despair doesn't have to be.

---

9. Ibid., p.172

10. Jansson, Tove. *Moominland Midwinter.* Translated by Ernest Benn, Square Fish, 2010, p.19

Moshe Schaffzin (they/them) is a writer of environmental fiction, poetry, essay and drama. Their work has appeared in *Kelp Journal, The Wave* and the University of Guelph's *Kaleidoscope Magazine*. They live and work in Guelph, Ontario, Canada with their cat.

A Rubāʿī for the rescued pangolin of Ravi flood

Fatima E.

Carried like wreckage on restless currents,
a hushed syllable of scales and fear adrift on brown water.
But a stranger's hands became a shore: gathered him whole.
The flood itself seemed to bless the act and surrendered him to hope.

Fatima E. is an architect by profession and a writer by inclination, whose work often explores the intersections of place, memory, and humanity. She is drawn to words that seek to bridge the distance between lived realities and the way they are remembered or retold. At home, her cat faithfully supervises every draft.

You can find her on Instagram: @whirlingmoonlight.

When the Earth Answers

Gloria Ogo

They say the first garden grew from the bones
of a forgotten city
steel girders rusting beneath lavender roots,
grief softened by moss.
We walked barefoot where highways once hissed,
the asphalt split by wild carrots
and the stubborn fists of dandelions.
Children played in the skeleton of a bank,
counting stones as currency.
No one missed the strums of machines.
We had learned to listen to other sounds
the murmur of water through reed,
the hush of leaves retelling stories
we thought we had lost.
We built our homes from what the sea spared:
driftwood, shells, glass made round with age.
Roofs that welcomed rain.
Windows shaped to honor the arc of sun.
Some of us still dreamed in fossil fuel,
woke sweating from the noise of combustion.
But even then, the bees returned
drunk on citrus and sage
reminding us of sweetness.
We no longer feared silence.
We let it gather
in the hollows of our throats
until we could speak again without poison.
And when the earth finally answered
not in thunder,
but in bloom
we promise never to forget
that it had always been trying
to love us back.

Gloria Ogo is an American-based Nigerian writer with several published novels and poetry collections. Her work has appeared in *Eye to the Telescope*, *Brittle Paper*, *Spillwords Press*, *Metastellar*, *Gypsophila Magazine*, *Harpy Hybrid Review*, *Allegro Poetry Magazine*, *CON-SCIO Magazine*, and more. With an MFA in Creative Writing, Gloria was a reader for *Barely South Review*. She is the winner of the Brigitte Poirson 2024 Literature Prize, the finalist for the Jerri Dickseski Fiction Prize 2024 and the ODU 2025 Poetry Prize, both with honorable mentions. She is also a finalist for Lucky Jefferson's 2025 Poetry Contest. Her work was longlisted for the 2025 American Short(er) Fiction Prize. https://glriaogo.wixsite.com/gloria-ogo.

Our Earth, Our Future

Oladosu Michael Emerald

Oladosu Michael Emerald (he/him) is a writer, artist, and an actor. He is the author of "Every Little Thing That Moves," an art editor at *Surging Tide* magazine and editor at *MAAR Review*. Instructor at The Arnheim Art Gallery, Young Artists Art Hub, and The Anasa Collection. He is the winner of the Off the Limit Art Contest (2024), Sprinng Poetry Contest (2024), Garden Party Collective Neurodivergent Poetry Contest (2025), and Sine Qua Non Inaugural Poetry Prize (2025). He's works published or forthcoming in *Chestnut Review*, *FIYAH*, *Lolwe*, *Temz Review*, and elsewhere. He is the Pioneer Fellow of the Muktar Aliyu Art Residency. Follow him on Twitter @garricologist and Instagram @garrycologist.

Sturgeon Baby

Sophie Fink

She was old
when the triceratops
first rammed their horns
into the trees that became soil,
became ice, became soaring steel
and concrete prisons, became ruins,
became swamp. Becoming herself had
been a beautiful thing: little egg sisters
slipping from their mother's folds, into the
cool waters of a lake far more dead than she
was. Sturgeon live mighty in quiet times—a hundred years or more
—and she had been ancient even before her death. Such a being to behold: her
slick pectoral fins; her sinuous barbells; her razor scutes. / Such an idea, her passing.
Long before the comet, the glaciers, the humans. Her corpse, wisping away, and her, left
behind, a remnant   of a lake so cold and pure and beautiful her idea of a heart   aches for it still.
This swamp is   not her home. This swamp is warm. Tangled. Steel beams   wrapped in
thorned vines and here her larvae, or someone's larvae,
play. / She watches them, these nascent sturgeon, as
they dart below a water-lily, mingle in a plastic cup.
They will grow here, die here, become ghosts here,
perhaps. She guides them, when she can. Away
from the alligator with the radioactive gums.
Through the cracked windows where the new

mayflies sleep. She loves them, in her own
idea of a way. / Sturgeon live desperate in
dying times. She watched so many dissolve:
flesh become bones become dust become
air. Become nothing, or the idea of nothing,
or something that perhaps never was. She
aches for them all, the dead and the dying.
She remembers herself through them, their snouts
as soft, their bellies as gentle as her own had been. She'd
let them live forever, if she could. She'd let them
swallow the earth. / The idea of her
is seven feet long. She curls around
her larvae, begs them to feed upon
her dreams. This swamp is their
home. She is their mother, their
father, their ghost. They are
beautiful, together, the idea
of her wrapped in the idea
of her children, the idea
of a lake, the idea
of a future brighter
and more alive
than anything
ever possible
before.

Sophie Fink holds a BA in English and creative writing from Colby College, and calls Minnesota home. She is currently pursuing an MLitt in Fantasy Literature at the University of Glasgow, with a particular interest in deep time narratives. Her work can also be found in *Strange Horizons*.

www.ingramcontent.com/pod-product-compliance
Lightning Source LLC
LaVergne TN
LVHW041153040626
840414LV00034B/413

* 9 7 8 1 9 5 5 3 6 0 1 4 2 *